26 Days with Saddam Hussein
The Interview before His Death

26 Days with Saddam Hussein
The Interview Before His Death

by
Chris Ford

Dedicated To

To All My Friends & Comrades Who Server Proudly In
The United States Military Police Corps.

Acknowledgements

First and foremost I wish to thank the United States Army, the Military Police Corp, the Military Secret Police, the Secret Service, the Department of Justice, the CIA, the FBI, the NSA, the Iraqi Government, Family Members of Saddam Hussein and a Handful of American Congressmen and Senators who will remain nameless and whom I had to pull some strings to be able to get permission to publish this book. Without the help of these people and contacts this book would have never been possible. For this I am eternally grateful.

Also I want to thank SSA. G.L.Piro for asking very good questions to President Hussein. Much of his investigation and findings have gone into this publication.

Preface

I guess the only way to start this will be, letting you know that I still to this day am nobody special. I don't claim to be better than anybody else. And I definitely don't claim to be better than the soldiers who have given their lives for their countries both American and Iraqi. I am however very fortunate to have met quite a few very important people throughout my military career. As a forensic psychologist in the United States Army Military Secret Police, it was my job to psychologically analyze high profile criminals. And in my whole career, I never anticipated nor did I ever dream that one day I would sit across the table from then ousted Iraqi President Saddam Hussein Abd al-Majid al-Tikriti.

The execution of Saddam Hussein took place on Saturday the 30th of December 2006. Pres. Saddam Hussein was sentenced to death by hanging, after being found guilty and convicted of crimes against humanity by the Iraqi special Tribunal for the murder of 158 Iraqi Shiites in a town of Dujail in 1982, this was in retaliation for an assassination attempt against him.

Saddam Hussein was the president of Iraq from 16 July 1979 to 9 April 2003 when he was overthrown during the 2003 military invasion. Saddam was found hiding in a hole on December 13, 2003 with approximately $700,000 American cash on his person. He was immediately taken and incarcerated at Camp Cropper and on November 5, 2006 he was sentenced to death by hanging.

On November 10, 2006 I was given direct orders by a Military Tribunal to sit with Pres. Saddam Hussein and understand, or try to understand what his reasoning and thinking was during the tenure of his dictatorship presidency and why he did the things he did. Additional to pick his brain and find out the ever so famous million dollar questions of as to where he was hiding the "Weapons of Mass Destruction". I spent 26 days with this man, asking him question after question after question. My job was to get to know him, understand him, and report everything that he told me.

This book chronicles the entire interview with SSA Piro that was conducted with Pres. Saddam Hussein. Every question and every answer is exactly as he replied. As well as a small chitchat that took place before during and after interviews, even when as he got irritated at me for asking the same questions over again but phrased differently is transcribed and printed in this book. All recordings that were made were taken and sealed by the United States Government. But they did not take from me my personal notes from which this book is derived from. After the interview was completed I asked Pres. Hussein to read them and to please verify to me if what I had written down was true and correct. Of the 300 or so pages of notes that I do have he read every page and autographed the back of my notes and told me that he was proud that I got it correct and that the world and his beloved people will know exactly what had taken place.

I find myself more fortunate than a world news reporter because I was allowed to ask any question and write it down exactly as it was stated with no sugar coating. Some of you will not want to believe what I'm writing. And that's okay that's your prerogative. But I tell you now I can only put down what was said to me or what is in the archives of history. There are some things that were said to me that will really infuriate political people within the boundaries of United States of America. This is probably why the recordings were taken.

I welcome any input or questions from any of you who possess this book. You must remember this is history, and history is something that we cannot change. The only thing we must try to do is never repeat what we have seen or what we have done.

I learned a lot in my time with him, I learned that life is too short. I learned that we should not take for granted the things that are special to us. Because in one day no matter how big we are or how protected we think we are, life's mysteries can all come crashing down on you in a second, and you would never see it coming.

This book will give you the insight into the mind of an Islamic President. In the 25 plus year reign as the Iraqi military commander-in-chief. And I leave it up to you to pass the judgment as to his guilt or innocence. Keep in mind that he was not tried or executed for any other thing except the people that he killed in retaliation for his assassination attempt.

I believe when we sit in a rocking chair at night on our front porch, and we contemplate the fact that someone has tried to kill us, our own self-preservation would kick in. If you knew the people who were trying to kill you, the obvious answer is to get them before they get you. Especially if they failed two different times. Pres. Saddam Hussein was executed for that exact reasoning. Not for the other violent acts that he did do throughout his 25 plus years as president. As with some of the actions that took place while he was the president of Iraq far outweigh the capture and murder of 158 would be assassins, as he did far worse things during his administration and did admit to. I believe the whole time I was taking notes and writing what he told me that he was telling the absolute truth. . As he had nothing to gain by lying to me. And he wanted the Iraqi people and the world to know the truth. I promised his family, (even though I should not have, but a man who is about to be executed does have the right to one last request whether he is a dictator, killer, terrorist or just a plain Joe.) that when I was able to release this information to the world that I would do so in the most respectful and reverent way possible as per his wishes.

Chapter 1

First Meeting

Saddam Hussein (High-Value Detainee #1) was interviewed on November 13, 2006 at a military detention facility at Baghdad International Airport, Baghdad, Iraq. Pres. Saddam Hussein provided the following information:

Pres. Hussein stated he had served the Iraqi people for a very long time. He considers his greatest accomplishments to be the social programs for the citizens of Iraq and improvements in other sectors of the economy including enhancements to the education, the health care system, industry, agriculture, and other areas that generally enhance the way of life for Iraqis.

In 1968, Iraqi people "Barely had anything." Food was scarce, both in rule villages as well as in cities. Farmland was neglected and agricultural methods were primitive. The Iraqi economy depended entirely on oil production, with most being exported from Iraq by foreign companies and not controlled by the government. As the country of Iraq manufactured very few products, most goods had to be imported. The health care system was "primitive" and the mortality rate was very high, particularly among the poor. The infant mortality rate was very high, estimated at 40 – 50 percent, with many deaths occurring during pregnancy or delivery. The literacy rate was around 27 percent with those classified as "literate" often not capable of true proficiency in either skill. Roads were almost nonexistent in rule areas and "very bad" and the cities of Iraq. Limited education opportunities existed at the university level, even

1

in Baghdad. Many cities had no college whatsoever generally, only wealthy individuals could afford to send their children to a university.

Pres. Hussein improved all the areas. Discussed. He considers this is greatest accomplishments and "service" to the Iraqi people.

In response to the questions regarding Pres. Hussein's own mistakes, Hussein agreed that all humans make mistakes, and only God is free of error. He noted that I was "smart" and it appeared that he had read reports from Hussein's previous interviews. Hussein stated, "Perhaps, a conversation between two such educated people will not be useful or successful." If one says he is perfect, he is saying he is like God. Pres. Hussein added that not all of his efforts were viewed as successful in some of the people's eyes. Hussein compared this evaluation of himself by others and the existence of the furring viewpoints to his own views about the American system of government, of which he is "not convinced." He pointed out that approximately 30,000,000 people live in poverty in America, but US residents do not consider this a "crime." Pres. Hussein stated he would never accept that for Iraq. When prompted by myself a second time regarding Hussein's own mistakes, he asked, "Do you think I would tell my enemy if I made a mistake?" Pres. Saddam Hussein stated that he would not identify mistakes he had made to an enemy, like America. He pointed out that he does not consider me an enemy, nor the American people, but the American system of government.

Hussein stated it is not only important what people say or think about him now but what they think in the future, 500 or thousand years from now. One of the most important things, however, is what God thinks. If God believe something, he will convince the people to believe. If God does not agree, it does not matter what the people think. Hussein added that a "traitor" provided information which led to his capture. As a "guest" at the location and as an Iraqi, he should not have been given up to the US forces. The grandchildren of this "traitor" will hold him accountable and tell this to future generations.

In the future, Saddam Hussein believes he will be known for fairness and as having "faced oppression." Ultimately, what the Iraqis think will be up to them. Hussein stated Iraqis would not compare leaders of the pre-Islamic era to the Islamic era.

Hussein believes Iraqi citizens were able to exercise their rights to Self-Govern as guaranteed by the Interim constitution in 1990. This occurred because the people had a leader and the government to lead them.

Hussein believes Iraq "will not die." Iraq is a great nation now, as it has been at times throughout history. Nations generally "go to the top" only once. Iraqi, however, has been there many times, before and after Islam. Iraqi is the only nation like this in the history of the world. This "gift" was given to the Iraqi people by God. When Iraqi people fall, they rise again. Hussein believes the Iraqi people "will take matters into their own hands," rule themselves, and, with God, decide what is right. Hussein hopes that Iraq will advance in all areas, finance, religious, etc. he added that, as a humanitarian, he hoped the same for the American people.

Hussein like to quote passages from the book "Zabibah and the King," commonly attributed as his writing, where the deputy shout, "Long Live Zabibah! Long live the people. Long live the Army." The deputies do not, however, shall "Long live the King." I asked

Hussein whether the Iraqi people will forget or failed to shout for him, to which he replied "No." He said, "It's in God's hands." Hussein emphasize the King is not the main subject of the book, rather the people. He stated God comes first, then the people. Hussein added Jesus Christ was considered "from the people" as Mary was of the people in Christ lived among the people. Being faithful is a cherished thing in life, being a traitor is the worst thing. Hussein stated, "God wanted to tell us don't be surprised when people are traitors to you." Hussein and did this portion of the discussion by saying "a prisoner cannot do anything for the people." He said he still has to have faith in God and repeated "it's in God's hands."

Hussein stated the National Progressive Front, a political Party, first existed as the National Front from 1970 – 1974. The national front consisted of the Kurdistan Democratic Party (KDP), the Communist Party, and the Ba'ath Party. Political parties express differences in Iraq as occurs in other countries. Some groups, including the Kurds, did not believe in socialism along the same ideological lines as the Ba'ath Party. In 1991, the National Progressive Front never actually came into power because of failure to pass the Constitution which was due to the first Gulf War.

Hussein considered any individual who was faithful to Iraq, and to the people, to be part of the Ba'ath. The Ba'ath takes responsibility for the success and mistakes. In 1989 and again in 2002, Hussein attempted, unsuccessfully, to convince his "colleagues" of the necd for multiple political parties in Iraq. And Hussein's opinion, one Party was not good for Iraq. Hussein stated, "Life does not accept only one idea. It accepts only one God." Hussein continued saying that a political system similar to Americans, with multiple parties, would cause "too much commotion" for the Iraqi people and they would have to be forced to accept it. Hussein said, "I wish there were parties other than the." Differences, from family through the people to the government, are good. Hussein ended this portion of the discussions by stating, "currently, the only political parties exist in Iraq are the ones with the weapons."

Hussein started quoting another passage from "Zabibah and the King" which states, "I am a great leader. You must obey me. Not only that, you must love me." I then asked him if a leader can obtain greatness through his achievements for his people or demand greatness through fear. Hussein responded that fear will not make a rule and will not make people love it will. Love comes through communication. The "author" of this book is comparing this King to pass Kings. He did not want to emphasize or advocate the idea of a monarchy to the people as the "author" does not approve of this form of government. Thus, the king died and Zabibah lived, as a symbol of the people.

Hussein believes people will love him more after he passes away than they do now. People are resisting the occupation of Iraq, now and before, under the "banners" of Hussein. Now, however, Hussein is not in power and is in prison.

Pres. Hussein stated people love someone for what they have done. During his presidency and before, he accomplished much for Iraq. He concluded a peace agreement with Barzani (the Kurds) in the north in 1970. Hussein nationalized the Iraqi oil industry in 1972. He supported the 1973 war against Israel in Egypt and Syria. Iraq survived eight years of war with Iran from 1980 – 1988 and the first Gulf War shortly thereafter. Iraqi live through 13 – 14 years of a boycott. And then as a joke he asked me if the boycott still existed, and I totally know. Despite all the hardships of issues under direct, one hundred percent of the people voted for Hussein in the last elections. And Hussein's opinion, they still supported their leader.

One things Saddam Hussein told me I thought was kind of funny was that the farm where he was captured in December 2003 was the same location he stayed in 1959 after fleeing Baghdad upon participating in a failed assassination attempt on then the Iraqi President Qassem actually we both found that amusing.

Chapter 2

The Iranian War

President Hussein was asked whether the decision to go to war against Iran in September, 1980 was based on the threats from Iran or whether the war was a means to reclaiming Arab/Iraqi territory, specifically the Shatt-al-Arab Waterway. Hussein stated, "We consider the war as having started on September 4, not September 22, as the Iranian state." Hussein then provide an example of a farmer who is your neighbor next door. Hussein prefers to use farming/rule examples as they have special meaning to him. One day, the neighbor's son beat up your son. The next day, the neighbor's son bothers your cows. Subsequently, the neighbor's son damages your farmland by disturbing the irrigation system. If all these things have occurred, eventually, after enough incidents, you approach your neighbor, tell him each transgression by event and ask him to stop. Usually, a warning or approach to the neighbor is enough to stop this behavior. With Iran, however, this approach by Iraq did not work. Iran, in Hussein's opinion, was in violation of the 1975 "Algiers Agreement" concerning the waterway. Furthermore, I ran was also deemed to have interfered in Iraq he politics, also a violation of the treaty. And Hussein's opinion, this left Iraq note choice but to fight. Thereafter, erect for the war in sacrifice so that interference by Iran in Iraq would end.

Pres. Hussein provided me some thoughts about the mindset of the Iranian leadership, specifically the Ayatollah Khomeini, and the Iranian decision to fight the war. When Khomeini came to power in

7

1979, he had two things which "interfere" with his mind. One, he was a religious fanatic who thought all leaders were like the Shah of Iran, a person easily toppled. Khomeini thought since he removed the shah so easily he could do the same elsewhere including Iraq second, Khomeini had a "complex" about leaving/being kicked out of Iraq previously in the late 1970s. Khomeini, exiled from Iran, had been a "guest" of Iraq who was "given shelter" in Najaf. While there, he began speaking out against the Shah and the Iranian government. Khomeini, and Hussein's opinion, was not respecting the written agreement (Algiers Agreement) go to the between Iraq and Iran and was interfering in internal Iranian affairs. The Iraqi government informed Khomeini of their position. They also told him "you are our guests, no one can ask you to leave or for you to be handed over." The Shah had, in fact, trying to get Hussein to turn over Khomeini to Iran. In Arab culture, one cannot "give up" a guest.

Khomeini refused to cease his activities against the Shah and the Iranian government. Khomeini stated that if his practices were against Iraqi policy, he would leave. Thereafter, he attempted to depart to Kuwait but was refused entry. Iraqi allowed him to return for three or four days income plied with his requests for assistance in traveling to another country. Khomeini then traveled to Paris, France.

Hussein stated that he does not regret it Iraq's treatment of Khomeini. When asked whether Khomeini ignored the gratitude of Iraq upon return from Kuwait, a step which could have resulted in Iraq's refusal to admit him and subsequent transfer to Iran, Hussein said, "no. It would not have changed the situation. The people did not want the Shah." Khomeini became a symbol for the people of Iran after departing Iraq because of his age and because he had been "kicked out" of Iran. Hussein only stated "maybe" when questioned whether Ayatollah Sayed Mohammed Sadr, a prominent Shia cleric executed in Iraq in 1980, may have been such a symbol. The same added he himself was a symbol as one could find pictures of Hussein inside houses and elsewhere in Iraq.

Khomeini believed the Shia population in southern Iraq would follow him, especially during the war with Iraq. But, according to the saying, "they did not welcome him." In fact, the Shia remain loyal to Iraq and fought the Iranians.

Hussein acknowledged that the Iranian military in 1980 was weak and "whacked leadership" as most of the high – ranking officers have been removed upon change of the Iranian leadership from the Shah to Khomeini. This, however, did not impact the decision to engage in war with Iran at that moment. Hussein stated, "If the Shah's army still existed, we would have defeated them in the first month." Under Khomeini, despite lacking leadership, the Iranian military, including the Army and the Revolutionary guard, "advanced in the thousands" against Iraq he forces. The Iraqi army fought bravely, especially at the borders.

I asked Hussein whether assassination attempts against Iraqi government officials prior to the conflict, allegedly at the of the Iranian – backed groups, including Foreign Minister Tyriq Aziz and Minister of Culture in Information Latif Nayyif Aziz, Affected the decision to go to war with Iran. Hussein stated that there were "540 assaults" on Iraq by Iran before the war. 249 of those "assault" included air incursions or raids. Iraq presented this information to the United Nations. Iran blocked the shot out Rob waterway and sank Iraq he and foreign ships. Before September 29, 1980 Iran bombed Iraq E oil refineries in Basra and other cities in southern

Iraq. The assassination attempts against Aziz and Jasim, and others, were up among the many incidents leading up to the war with Iran.

I asked him the objective of this war, and Hussein replied, "Ask Iran. They began the war. I have explained all the reasons for the war before." Upon repeating the question, Hussein stated the object was "To have Iran not interfere in our internal affairs." Hussein repeated some information previously provided including the fact that he believed Iran violated the treaty of 1975 (Algiers Agreement). Iran occupied the entire Shatt-al-Arab Waterway, while the agreement stated their right to only half. Iran did not respond to the diplomatic communications regarding these facts.

Hussein stated Iraqi forces initially succeeded in occupied cities and territories in southern Iran just across the border including areas in and near Muharma, Ahwaz, and Dosful. Iraqi forces did not push further into Iran because the immediate objective was to stop artillery attacks from Iran which emanated from areas near the border.

After approximately 2 years, Iraqi forces were pushed back in the war became defensive and for Hussein's military. I asked him why the war became defensive for Iraq. Hussein stated that "One cannot plan for the Iraqi army the same as one for the American Army." From a military viewpoint, plans are made according to capabilities. The military agrees that when supply routes are linked in, problems arise. Hussein stated, "T hello he soldier of today is not the same as the soldier of 100 years ago." They are part of a "universal group" hearing and seeing things on the television and radio. The soldier is "part of the world" and is "affected" by this. If order to counter attack, the "winning" soldier will pushed to the objective and beyond. Hussein agreed that the later Iraqi offensive stage of the war in 1986 – 87 solved many successes, including the capture of three quarters of Iranian tanks and half of the artillery and armored personnel carriers.

Hussein discuss further the reasoning behind not advancing further into Iran. He repeated that Iraqi had receive enough territory, removing the threat of Iranian artillery, in the early years of the war. Hussein said, "If we went deep inside Iran, they would think we wanted something else." He added, "We did not face a regular army, which is easier to plan against." Hussein further stated that for many Iraqi soldiers, this was their first combat experience. Many were "pumped up" especially with the early successes into Iranian territory. Within a few days, however, many soldiers thought "why am I here?" As confirmed in a saying by the Iraqi military leaders many soldiers preferred to defend the borders and remain in Iraq. Withdrawal of Iraq he forces from Iranian territory should have occurred before this change in mentality took place. Some of the military commanders wanted to remain, others wanted to withdraw. After two years of war, some Iraqi military leaders felt Iran had "learned its lesson" and recommended withdrawal. Hussein respected information from the military commanders and ordered withdrawal of the Iraqi forces.

Hussein stated, normally, defensive operations are not "good from a technical standpoint" nor are they good for the soldiers "morale". Pres. Hussein said "if a soldier does not see logic, he will not perform as well or be obedient. If he accepts the task at hand as logic, he will be obedient. A soldier must be convinced, otherwise discipline is a problem." Hussein commented about the present of mental state of American soldiers in Iraq. He said "if you asked the American soldier, who came to Iraq to find weapons of mass destruction, but none could be found, and who came to remove the leaders of the Hussein dictatorship, who are all in jail now, but are replaced with other dictators, whether he wanted to stay or go, he would say go."

When asked whether the use of chemical weapons by Iraq against Iran during the defensive. Of the war occurred only through necessity, i.e., Iraq would have lost the war without such use, Hussein responded, "I do not have an answer for that. I am not going to answer." When asked whether he thought Iraq was going to lose the war with Iran, particularly after 1982 and during the 1984 – 86 timeframe, Hussein responded, "no. Not for a second. I said this on television. I said this in five letters I sent to Iran." In the letters, Hussein outlined the strengths of the Iraqi military. Hussein stated some Iraqi commanders did not like the fact that this type of information was included and letters to Iran. Iranian leaders thought Hussein was lying, while Iraqis believed him. Returning to Iraq chemical weapons use, Hussein stated "I will not be cornered or caught on some technicality. It will not do you any good. The United States has paid dearly for its mistakes here in Iraq and throughout the world and will continue to pay for its mistakes all over the world as long as they continue to get involved in and mettle in the Arabian/Islamic cultures."

Hussein stated Iran did not "get the message" after 1982 when Iraq pullbacks to its borders. He stated, "If you do not break their heads, they will not understand."

Hussein stated Iraqi, "did not owe much money" after the war with Iran. Iraqi had received aid from a rev countries, which Hussein believed to be and not loans. After the war, however, these countries "change their minds" and demanded repayment. Some countries viewed Iraq as a military threat. Iran was not viewed as a military threat, as its forces were devastated by the war. Hussein laughed at this point.

Hussein stated Iraqi agreed to the United Nations resolution on September 28, 1980 calling for a secession of hostilities with Iran. Iran, however, did not agree to this resolution. Hussein added that Iraqi also agreed to UN resolution 598 in 1987 calling for an end to the war. In Iran, again, did not agree to this resolution either. Iraq, in fact, attempted numerous times throughout the war to engage Iran and discussions in order to stop the fighting. Hussein stated "we did this when we did not have to" for the good of the people and for humanity. Iran only except in terms of cease-fire in 1988 "after they lost the war."

Regarding UN findings about Iraq's use of chemical weapons during the Iran – Iraq war, Hussein stated, "History is written and will not change. No one can stop history from being written." Hussein pointed out that your brand used chemical weapons first, at Muharma (which is Khorramshahr in Iraq), in September/October, 1981. When asked whether Iraqi had to use chemical weapons for defensive reasons, Hussein responded, "I am not going to answer, no matter how you put the question."

Hussein stated, "I will discuss everything unless it hurts my people, my friends, or the Army." Hussein gave details of the incident 1964 involving Ahmad Hasan Al-Bakr, general secretary of the Ba'ath Party. Bakr and Hussein, who was chief of the military branch of the bath at that time, were arrested for plotting a coup against then Iraqi President Aref. Hussein stated he admitted full responsibility for the plot and could not have provided information against anyone else.

Hussein stated, "It is not fair for someone in charge to blame others. If someone says Saddam told me to do it, which is not a problem for me and does not hurt me."

Chapter 3

The Palestinian Situation

President Hussein provided his comments regarding the Palestinian situation. Any attempt to understand the roots of the problems surrounding the Palestinian issue should be made from the viewpoint of an Arab, and not just a Palestinian. The problem is not only a Palestinian one but also a rev one in the 1960s, many revolutions occurred in a rev countries with the uprisings generally taking place as a result of the dissatisfaction of the people with the rulers of those times. Part of the reason leaders were removed was their failure to address the Palestinian issues adequately or ignoring it altogether. Any solution to the problem should be based on fairness and international law. International law, and its application, created the problem in 1948 upon formation of the separate Jewish state of Israel from lands previously claimed by the Palestinians. A solution, from foreigners and those "internal" to the issue, must be presented in that scope. Everyone has been looking for solution. However, Hussein stated, "a solution were that does not convince the majority of the Palestinians will not be successful." The foundation of any such solution, and the final outcome, must be the establishment of a separate state of Palestine.

When I questioned him about a speech he once gave regarding the 1968 Revolution in Iraq, Hussein agreed that he commented in the speech "we did not revolt against the person who voted against the system of government." He further agreed that he's dated the revolution was undertaken "to move Iraqi people, the country, the

15

Arab world as a whole, and the Palestinians forward." Hussein also added that the Ba'ath Party was the only political Party that demonstrated against the Iraqi government in 1967.

I asked him about the six-day a wrap – Israeli war in 1967, Hussein stated the rats hope the lands lost in 1948 would be one back. Hussein stated "we were sad when that did not happen." Although expectations were low for success, the news was especially disheartening when details were provided about the rapid defeat of the Egyptians and Syrian military force. People of the Arab world became "sad and depressed" and developed a feeling of revolution.

Even though the 1967 war was lost by Iraqi, Hussein still respected Egyptian president Gamal Abdel Nasser after the war. In Hussein's opinion, Nasser "Could represent the Arabs to the world" while others were "weak." At that time, Nasser was the only ruler with the close relationship to the "Arab Masses". Despite losing the war, Nasser did not lose the respect of the people. The hopes of the people, however, were greater than the result Nasser could deliver. Losing the war showed the limits and capabilities of Nasser and the Egyptian Military Forces. Hussein pointed out that the war also exposed internal issues in the Egyptian leadership. Abdul Hakim Ammer, head of the Egyptian military, would not permit nesters "interference" in military matters "even though nasty air was head of the country." When necessary later resigned millions of Egyptians protested for him to resume his duties as president. Hussein opinion that it seemed "necessary depended on international politics rather than preparation of his military and people" leading up to the war. When he died in 1970, citizens "cried for him."

Regarding the 1973 Arab – Israeli war, Egyptian Pres. Sadat, who served as vice president under Nasser "could not bring back the hopes of the Arabs." Sadat seem not to have a specific cause or a team and was unable to do anything about 1948 and the "rape of Palestine." Because Sadat was not a "man of cause," Egyptian soldiers were not "motivated" by him. Similarly, the people of Egypt were not motivated. In fact during this time, Egyptians mocked their own soldiers making jokes about the military saying they did not fight in 1967. Sadat did, however, this was his own personality, make the United States and Israel believed he could win a war with Israel.

I questioned him about Sadat's ability to ultimately do more for his people than Nasser, particularly with respect to bringing peace and reclaiming territory, Hassan stated Nasser's effect was "nominal." "Nominal." Hussein added, "If you tell Iraqis Kuwait will be a part of Iraq, they will be happy." The Arab nation, from poor to wealthy individuals, is one nation with the same language, common borders, and the same aims. There is one Arab world, from the "simple person to the lawmakers and thinkers." The strengths of any person in a "family" comes from corporations with and love of each other in the "family." If a member of the "family" does not understand this, he will be "weak and fall." Sadat was not faithful to "family" matters. Prior to the 1967 war, the West Bank and Jerusalem were under control of Jordan while Gaza was under control of Egypt. Sadat's peace agreement with the Israelis failed to return the territories to the rightful owners, the Palestinians. Thus, Sadat was a "traitor to the cause." Israel only willingly returned this Sinai Peninsula as it was a "military burden" and was an easy "political move." Sadat lost honor as a result of agreements made with Israel. Additionally, the Egyptian economy worsened significantly under his leadership. In contrast, Egypt's economy flourished under Nasser with its markets open to all Arab countries.

President Hussein stated, quote being at peace is not easy." Piece without a cause will create a change in balance. Regarding eight comment made to a British journalists or possibly two years ago, Hussein did not mean peace could be achieved by losing faith and present age. On the contrary, any piece should be negotiated to a "favorable position of power."

Pres. Hussein stated Iraqi file in the 1973 war on two fronts, with its air force contributing to Egypt and Syria and the ground forces fighting in Syria. When asked whether Iraqi could have done more, Hussein responded, "what more could we have done? We sent all our military to fight under Egyptian and Syrian command." Prior to the war, Egypt had sent then vice president Mubarak to Iraq to request aircraft and pilots for use in attacking Israeli surface to air missile sites. Iraq provided the aircraft though they were already fighting the Kurds in the north. The Syrians requested Iraqs assistance just after start of the war saying Israel would occupy Syria without Iraqs help.

Regarding the reported failure of the Syrian military to "openly welcome" Iraqi forces in 1973, Hussein stated, "no one is as generous as Iraqis." Hussein was further asked for his comments regarding the failure/refusal of the Syrian military to provide Iraqi forces with maps, communications equipment, and other assistance needed to fight the war together. Hussein replied, "A loser does not know where his head and his feet are. It was a difficult situation, to come together like this." Hussein postulated, "Perhaps the Syrians did not have maps." Iraqi officers were accustomed to different treatment in their own military ranks.

Iraqi has always accepted Palestinian refugees into the country, during Hussein's time and previously. These influxes of refugees include after 1948 upon formation of Israel after September, 1970 (Black September in Jordan), and in 1991 after the first Gulf War. Hussein stated, "We welcome them, gave them jobs, and gave them the right to own land and a house." The latter policy regarding homes was in contradiction with his doctrine of the Arab League which did not permit Palestinians to own residences. In Hussein's opinion Arab League members assume that Palestinians would not leave if they own their own residences. Hussein did not agree with this policy for "humanitarian reasons." When presented by Hussein, the Iraqi leadership agreed with his position. For Palestinians in Iraq, "this help might be normal."

Hussein acknowledge that Iraqi government built and/or rented some homes for Palestinians for Iraqi landlords. Hussein stated, "We were concerned about everybody in Iraq. We would not have let them live in the streets. Things such as food, work and a home are needed for the sake of pride." Hussein stated some people accused Iraq of trying to remove the Palestinians. Hussein added, on the contrary, we "could not kick a guest out." In accordance to the Algiers Agreement.

Pres. Hussein did not remember whether the Iraqi government paid all or a portion of rent, for all or a certain amount of time, for the Palestinian housing in Iraq. Hussein has no knowledge of home owners suing the government for unpaid rent, particularly in the early to mid-1990s, and losing such a case to the government. Hussein stated, "If we promise to pay, we would have done it. If the case was lost, the government must not have promised to pay." Hussein denied there was a law permitting the government to "rent" homes without actually paying rent to the landlord. He said, "That's not true. There was no such law. That's rape ordered jungle law." Hussein asked to see the wall on paper.

The same provide comments about the 1974 Rabat Summit where it is reported that the Iraqi government gave up its belief in the "armed struggle" for Palestine and accepted a "phased strategy." Hussein stated that this was the first conference he had ever attended. Usually, the Iraqi Minister of foreign affairs attended on behalf of the government. At the summit, the Palestinian liberation organization (PLO) presented a general strategy asking Jordan for the West Bank as a homeland. Previously, the West Bank and Jerusalem were under control of Jordan and its ruler King Hussein. Hussein stated, "We approve this after a speech by King Hussein." In Hussein's opinion, King Hussein did not object to the plan "but seemed unconvinced." Also at this time, Iraq agreed that the PLO would be the only legal representative of Palestine.

Hussein acknowledged that Palestinian groups, including Al-Fatah, had offices in Baghdad. In 1978, however Al-Fatah closed its offices and reportedly dissed attributed leaflets. The same does not know the details of the message on the leaflets but heard it was negative towards the Iraqi government. The relationship between the Iraqi government and Al-Fatah "was not good." Regarding the objectives of the Palestinian organizations, which seem to differ from those of the PLO and Iraq, Hussein stated friction between individuals or groups regarding the same matter often resulted in differing ideas being put forth. According to Hussein, the Palestinians needed "central control." The individuals compromising the leadership of the various Palestinian groups were "not on the same page." As for the Iraq East, the leadership met and decided not to interfere in the internal affairs of the PLO. According to the provisions of the Algiers Agreement. Hussein stated it was decided that Iraqi way "help as we can." The Palestinians were told, however, the limitations of the Iraqi government. Thereafter, direction regarding Iraqi assistance to Palestinians, and limitations were provided to all Iraqi government sectors. Hussein described relations with the PLO during this period of 1978 to 2003 as "good."

Hussein stated representatives of the Palestine Liberation Front (PLF) and Abu Nidal Organization (ANO) were present in Iraq at times. Hussein stated "we accepted them as guest." They were directed not to conduct activities against Iraq and to refrain from terrorism. The PLF and the ANL members were told not to interfere and in turn will affairs of the PLO. At one point, that ANL was worn to seize terrorist activities.

Hussein acknowledge the presence of Mohammed Abbas, a.k.a. Abu Abbas, in Iraq at some point. Hussein did not admit to specifically assisting Abbas. He stated, "If we accept someone as a guest, we must help them. A guest cannot, however, demand what he wants for breakfast, lunch and dinner." Hussein reiterated that Iraqi considered the PLO as the official political organization for Palestine and all other groups were secondary.

Hussein was told the details of a videotaped meeting which took place approximately 2 years ago between Abbas and Tahir Jail Habbush, Director of the Iraqi Intelligence Service. At the meeting, Abbas requested Iraqi assistance, including money, training, weapons, and transportation, to carry out missions to attack Israel. Hussein was told that I has seen the videotape. Hussein was questioned as to whether these actions planned against Israel, constituted a legitimate defense of Palestine or terrorism, thereby exceeding the normal assistance provided to a guest. Hussein asked, "What did the Iraqi government do? If you have a recording, you know." Hussein stated that his position is one where attempts are made to regain all Arab lands, including those "raped and taken." He stated this is neither a secret nor it is something which brings shame. Hussein added, if Habbush and Abbas met, that's something else. We call for a military struggle to regain Arab lands. The principles are the same as that which we have talked about before." Hussein continued, "If Abbas asked for these things, it does not mean we gave them to him. If Abbas carry out any attacks in Israel, that means we helped him. If he did not, we did not help him." When told Abbas carry out attacks in Israel, Hussein replied "yes he did, but those occurred before asking us for assistance. That was his choice." Hussein stated, "At any time, we had the ability and the right to help in the struggle. I am not talking about Abbas, I'm talking about organizations and Palestine. Outsiders are not serious." Hussein asked for the answer provided by Habbush to Abbas. I had told Hussein money was provided to a boss but not as much as he requested. Hussein stated, "This is intelligence work. We have been open about Palestine."

Hussein was questioned whether assistance to Abbas would help achieve the goals of Palestinians or whether it would work against such aims. Hussein stated since he was a "young struggler" in the Ba'ath Party, he believed any organization should fight from the inside, not the outside. Per Hussein, any attempts from the outside are just "talk" and "not serious." Hussein suggested further details regarding Abbas could be obtained from Habbush or from further review of the videotape of the meeting between the two.

I question him with regard to the director of the IIS on whether or not they would meet without the approval of the Iraqi leadership to discuss such a matter with Abbas, Hussein replied, "does the American Director of Intelligence call President Bush every time before meeting someone? Hussein agreed that the president, in both the United States and Iraq, sets policy for all branches of government. Hussein stated, although Abbas reportedly asked the Iraqi IIS director for one – $2 million according to what I told him, he would not have given him even "$10,000" Hussein added, "any Palestinian who wanted to train and to go fight for Palestine, I said train him. Money and weapons are different from training." Because of sanctions against Iraq, the government could not offer as much assistance as previously provided. Hussein stated, "if the IIS had the ability, it is not wrong as long as the struggle is on the inside."

I question Hussein whether Iraqi stated position of recognition of the PLO as the sole representative of Palestine conflict with support provided to other groups and individuals including Abbas. Hussein responded, "I didn't say I helped Abbas. Don't put words in my mouth." Hussein added "I think the question should be in the context of the dialogue, not the interrogation." Hussein continued saying, "if the IIS help Abbas, and he fought for Palestine, that is not wrong. If a person says he wants to struggle against Israel, and that person is not officially representing Palestine, there is no conflict with the Iraqi policy." Hussein said with any such person who stated he wanted to "negotiate" would not be supported by Iraq as that is the role of Arafat and not the PLO.

at the end of the interview today, Pres. Hussein was asked about his movements when the hostilities began in March 2003 Hussein stated he remained in Baghdad until April 10 or 11th 2003 whereupon it appeared the city was about to fall to the Americans. Prior to his departure from Baghdad, he held a final meeting with the senior Iraqi leadership and told them "we will struggle in secret." Thereafter, he departed Baghdad can begin gradually "dispersing" his bodyguards, telling them they had completed their duty, so as

23

not to draw attention. "I paid them well and took good care of their families for what they did for me."

Chapter 4

The United Nations

I began the discussion by explaining that today's session would be a drill dialogue regarding the United Nations (UN) and various resolutions concerning Iraq as passed by the UN.

Hussein said, "Let me ask a direct question. I want to ask where, from the beginning of this interview process until now, has the information I have been giving been going to? For our relationship to remain clear, I would very much like to know." I told Hussein that I am a representative of the United States government, and that report from these interviews are no doubt being reviewed by many US government officials. These individuals may include the president United States. Hussein stated that he would have no reservation if others were "brought into" the process and that he "does not mind" if the information is published.

When questioned whether Hussein had ever used "body doubles" or those resembling him as he has been often discussed in books and other publications, he laughed and stated, "This is new be magic, not reality." Hussein added that it is very difficult for someone to impersonate another individual.

When questioned whether others in the Iraqi government, including his son Uday, had used "body doubles" as has been described in a book by an Iraqi man, Hussein denied any information regarding these reports. He stated, "I think my sons would not do this." Hussein added they might have considered such a tactic during war,

25

but not in peace. He never saw "body doubles" for either of his sons, during times of war or peace. Hussein asked rhetorically, "do not think I am getting upset when you mentioned my sons. I still think about them and the fact they died martyrs. They will be examples to everyone throughout the world." Both of his funds fought in the war against Iran in the 1980s, before "arriving at the normal age." They, and one other individual, are the only ones known to Hussein as having fought while "under aged."

During the Iran – Iraq war in the battle for the liberation of the Al – Faw Peninsula in 1987, Hussein and all of his immediate male relatives fought in this war. This was an important and decisive battle, a fact which was communicated by Hussein to all Iraqis. Hussein stated, "When I believe in principles, I believe in them fully, not partly, not gradually, but completely." Hussein added that God creates us, and only he decides what he is going to take us. Hussein ended this portion of his interview saying, "if you decide to publish a book be sure to write it in English as well as Arabic."

Upon revisiting the issue whether Hussein ever used "body doubles" he replied, "No, of course not."

We then turned the discussion of Hussein's views and/or opinions of the UN during the 1990s, beginning with the UN resolution 687. As I relayed the UN resolution 687 that called for Iraq to, among other things, declare the existence, if any, or to destroy, chemical or biological weapons, and agree to make no further attempt to manufacture or acquire such weapons. The resolution also called for Iraq to reaffirm its compliance with the Nuclear Nonproliferation Treaty. UNR 687 also detailed steps which Iraqi had to undertake in order to have UN sanctions against the country lifted. I specifically asked Hussein's about his decisions and rationale for these decisions with respect to UNR 687.

Hussein stated UNR 661, not UNR 687, is the first resolution in the 1990s concerning Iraq which would eventually contribute to tensions and lead to the most recent war with the United States. I confirmed his familiarity with this resolution was stated UNR 687 would be the starting point for this discussion.

Hussein acknowledge Iraqi accepted UNR 687. Hussein further acknowledge Iraqi made a mistake by destroying some weapons without UN supervision. When question as to whether Iraqi also made a mistake regarding failure to provide complete disclosure, initially and throughout the process, Hussein responded, "That's a very good question." UNR 687 was not written according to the "UN way." If followed UNR 661, issued before the first Gulf War, as similar to UNR 661, was supported by the United States. Hussein stated, "The United States started the cause and others followed. 661 was agreed upon by all parties while 687 was not."

After the first Gulf War began, the US president eventually requested a meeting in the Gulf on a ship, similar to the meeting held at the end of World War II between the United States and Japan, in order to discuss a cease-fire agreement. Iraqi refuse such a meeting. Ultimately, Iraqi met with leaders of other countries in a location "at the borders." Iraqi agreed to a cease-fire and withdrew its armies. Thereafter, UNR 687 was passed. Hussein reiterated that UNR 687 was approved at the insistence of the United States. According to the saying, "no such decision" existed before in the history of the UN.

When the first Gulf War began, Iraqi military forces were "away from the borders." There were those who wanted to "rape" Iraqi in war, since they could not do that in peace.

The Iraqi government wrote letters to the UN affirming compliance with UNR 687. Iraqi did not agree with the resolution but agreed to implement it so that "People would not get hurt."

In Hussein's view, US specters wanted all expenses, including their accommodations, travel, and other costs paid for by Iraq. Instead of waiting for the inspectors and bearing these expenses, erect commenced destruction of the weapons. Iraq did not hide these weapons. UN inspectors later requested documentation of the destruction of the weapons and visited various places taking samples for review. Hussein stated, "If it is presumed that we were mistaken in the percentage of weapons that we say we destroyed, then how many mistakes were made by the United States according to UNR 687?" These "mistakes" include occupying Iraq, implementation of the "No-Fly Zones" over northern and southern Iraq, and the bombing of Iraq which took place from the first Gulf War to the most recent one. Hussein question why the UN implemented UNR 687 in such a harsh manner against Iraq, other than UN resolutions, including those against Israel, were not enforced. Hussein ended this portion of the discussion saying, "If we were to bring a professor from a college in the United States to Iraq, he would agree with my observation regarding UNR 687, with the exception of the issue of the sovereignty of another country (Kuwait)."

During our lengthy dialogue regarding UNR 687, Hussein made several statements. He acknowledged that UNR 687 past and Iraq agreed "to deal with it." Regarding destruction of weapons, Hussein stated, "we destroyed them. We told you, with documents. That's it." When questioned about Iraqi restrictions placed on locations visited by UN inspectors, Hussein replied, "What places?" He was told numerous locations including the Ministry of agriculture, to which Hussein replied, "By God, if I had such weapons, I would have used them in the fight against the United States." I then pointed out that most accused persons who are innocent agree to a full and complete examination of the details of the accusation. Once cleared, the accused Party would then provide evidence of any mistreatment during the investigation. Hussein stated, "This is not a question, it is a dialogue. Good."

Hussein opinion that the United States used prohibited weapons in Vietnam. He asked whether America what accept Iraqis inspecting the White House for such weapons. Hussein stated any such search would likely find nothing. He added, "A country that except spume violated will bring dishonor to its people." Negotiation is the normal method of resolution of any disagreement, particularly among nations. Negotiation is the way "the way of the UN." Hussein asked "What country in the world used weapons of mass destruction and murdered 300,000 innocent people in one day?" It was evidently clear that Hussein was referring to the end of World War II when the United States dropped atomic bombs on Hiroshima and Nagasaki. Hussein emphasize that "those were innocent people." And that they had no way of defending themselves. And that United States is the only country to use weapons of mass destruction not only in World War II but as stated before Vietnam additionally.

When emphasized to Hussein that the international community agreed that Iraqi had not complied with UNR 687, he responded that Iraq believed there was something wrong with "the international way." The United States convince the world of its position regarding Iraq. Regarding further discussion, Hussein commented, "I must prepare an answer in my mind, so that it does not come in pieces. Let's leave the password is, not that we agree, but to maximize our time."

Hussein commented that in the most recent war with Iraq, the United States only how I was Britain. All other major countries, including France, China, Russia, and Germany, were against the war. The United States was "looking for a reason to do something." Now, the United States is here and did not find any weapons of mass destruction. Hussein pointed out to me that decisions were made by the Iraqi leadership and not just by Hussein. Iraqi leaders make decisions which gave the United States and "opening" and the reasons for the most recent war. Pres. Hussein remarked that, at times, people told Jesus Christ, the prophet Mohammed, Moses, David, and all other prophets to give up their beliefs, teachings, and principles to save their own lives. Hussein stated, "If a man gives up his principles, his life has no value. In the case of the profits, they would have been ignoring the orders of God." Hussein added, "If Iraq had given up its principles, we would have been worthless." Hussein stated that he was elected by the people, and not "brought in by some other country or companies." Thus, he was required to comply with the principles of the people.

I stressed to Hussein that Iraq's actions led to the implementation of UN sanctions. The Iraqi leadership's actions, and in some cases failure to act, compelled the UN to continue the sanctions. Hussein responded, "This is your opinion. I answered." He continued saying that it is difficult to give up "your nationality, your country, and your traditions." Hussein pointed out that perhaps that I and another American might think differently on the subject of Iraq.

Hussein said, "If I wanted to be a politician, I could. But, I do not like politicians or politics." When noted to the saying that some people would state he played politics with the UN, Hussein stated, "We abided totally by the UN decision." The United States should be blamed, not the UN. Hussein stated, "We are among the few remaining cavaliers."

Upon any examination of blame, I pointed out one must first look at the origins of the discord between Iraq and the world, the invasion of Kuwait. Hussein responded, "America had a plan with Kuwait to attack Iraq. We had a copy of the plan in our hands. If I had the (prohibited) weapons, would I have let United States forces stay in Kuwait without attacking? I wish the United States did not have the intention to attack Iraq.& When questioned whether the Iraqi invasion of Kuwait, which led to war with the United States, also precipitated the sanctions against Iraq, Hussein asked, "I ask you as an American, when did the United States stop shipments of grain to Iraq? In 1989. When did the United States contact European countries to boycott sales of technological equipment to Iraq? In 1989. The United States was planning to destroy Iraq, and intention published by Zionism and the effect of the Zionism on elections in the United States." This US "plan" was also influenced by countries located near Iraq, particularly Israel, which led viewed Iraq as a dangerous military threat upon conclusion of the Iran – Iraq war. Hussein stated, "I believe this with my whole heart."

I asked regarding Kuwait and the war, and Hussein stated, "it is difficult to avoid someone who was armed and standing outside your house unless you come out and shoot." As a Iraq is a small country, it was difficult to stop the United States the matter what steps were taken.

Leading up to the most recent war, the United States provided much "history" to the world regarding Iraq. Hussein stated, "It was difficult for me, or any honorable person, not to attempt to stop the United States from entering Iraq."

When asked regarding his personal observations versus his opinions as Pres. of Iraq, Hussein stated, "There is nothing I consider personal. I cannot forget my capacity as president. This is what I know and am convinced out. Thus, it is difficult to answer from a personal viewpoint. I cannot forget my role and principles for one second, and forget what I was."

I asked him again about his movements after the beginning of the war in March 2003. Hussein stated he was not in the Dora neighborhood of Baghdad on March 19, 2003 when it was bombed by coalition forces. Hussein added that he was not in this neighborhood in the 10 days before this attack or any time throughout the war. Hussein believes that coalition forces targeted this location because they mistakenly believed he was present.

I asked about his movements before the fall of Baghdad in April 2003, Hussein stated that success in movement of persons or equipment during wartime required knowledge of enemy capabilities as well as "our own capabilities." The person's closest to Hussein would direct him to "move this way or that way." When asked whether Hussein normally traveled in a black Mercedes before the war he stated, "Perhaps. We had all colors of Mercedes." Regarding whether he normally traveled in a long motorcade, Hussein stated, "I'll leave this for history."

Chapter 5

The Ba'ath Party

I mentioned to the saying that I understood that an attempted coup in 1973 was undertaken by a protégé of his, Nadhim Kazzar, director of the Ba'ath Party's security service and the Shi'a from the city of Al-Amarah. Hussein related that at this time, the Party did not know which members were Sunni or Shi'a Muslims or Christians. As an example, he pointed out that it was not until later that he learned that one of the Parties leaders, Tariq Aziz, was a Christian. The Party was successful because it related to the people, and, thus, no distinction was made on members based on their religion or ethnicity.

Hussein related that among the parties leadership that between 1958 – 63, very few members were Sunni. The secretary general was Shi'a from the city of Al-Nasiriyah. The same claim that when he attempted to assassinate Pres. Qassem in 1959, he knew nothing about the Sunnis and Shi'as. After the revolution, people began inquiring which members were Sunni and which were members were Shi'as. At the time, it was difficult to know because they were all mixed together. However, by 1968, nearly all Party members were Sunnis. Because the Party had previously operated secretly, few knew or cared about one's religion. However after the revolution, people in the government began talking more frequently about this issue. Many were concerned that promotions and demotions were being decided on the basis of one's sect or religious affiliation. Hussein stated, "You would be surprised to know that the secretary general of the Party and 1964 was Kurdish."

Hussein was asked about a perception that Nadhim Kazar was Hussein's "right-hand man" and that at one time, he was considered a threat to take over Pres. Bakr's regime. Hussein refuted this characterization by saying that he was not his right-hand man in the government and that each person has their own duties and responsibilities. He said that although Kazar was neither of revolutionary nor among the 70 individuals who took over the presidential palace, he was a good Party member and top individual while he was in prison.

Kazar was not convinced that the military would be good for the Ba'ath Party. He was influenced by the thoughts of Party members who split and believed in a communist socialist philosophy. Kazar considered the military members of the Party to be old-fashioned and a burden. Despite his perspective, however Kazar decided to remain with the Party. Hussein had no information whether Kazar had met with officials in Iran. He related that when Kazar's coup failed, Kazar fled to Iran but was arrested before he arrived at the border. Hussein said he did not want to talk "bad" about Kazar. He said that when Kazar "arrested" the Minister of Defense Hamad Shihab and the Minister of Interior Sa'dun Ghaydan, it was done easily and did not require a big plan.

While discussing Kazar, Hussein digressed and characterize this period as being the best time for Iraq because "we nationalized oil, settled oil disputes with the oil companies and invested money in Thoura City," which was later renamed, Saddam City.

According to Hussein, the psychology of the Ba'ath Party was to recruit young individuals at the beginning of their schooling such as when they were in elementary and secondary school. The Party seldom recruited members from colleges. Their philosophy was that they wanted a person they could mold to "grow" into the Party. In the 1950s and 1960s the Party accepted primarily young people in only a few older individuals. Some Party members such as Kazar question the allegiance of newer officers to the Ba'ath Party.

I mentioned to the saying that many people believe because Kazar's plan to kill Pres. Bakr went awry after Kazar learned that Pres. Bakr's plane had been delayed and then incorrectly assumed that his plot had been exposed. I then continued stating that Kazar kidnapped Ministers Shihab and Ghaydan as hostages and fled to the border of Iran where he was captured by Hussein. Hussein responded by saying, "your information is not specific. According to my information, Pres. Bakr's plane was not delayed, and his guards were awaiting his arrival." Hussein waited at the airport for Bakr and after Bakr arrived, he accompanied him to the Presidential Palace where the two drink tea together. Hussein later excused himself so that Bakr could visit with his family. Hussein was then driven by his staff through Baghdad. As they were driving, they heard an announcement on the police radio that a coup had been attempted by Ministers Shihab and Ghaydan. Because of the importance of this matter, Hussein pushed his driver to the side and proceeded to drive the car himself to his residence which was located near the President's residence. Near the gate of his residence, Hussein used a telephone to call Bakr who asked where Hussein was located because he had something very important to relate. Hussein answered he was nearby, and that he had heard the news. Hussein met with Bakr at his residence. Bakr told Hussein that Ministers Shihab and Ghaydan had attempted a coup, saying that he had tried calling Ministers Shihab, but received no answer. Hussein advised Bakr that he had an "intuition" about Kazar and believed it was Kazar who had attempted the coup, not the two Ministers. Hussein subsequently asked Bakr to call the Military Division and prepared to go after Kazar and "to hit him before he crossed the border into Iran."

Near the borders of Iran where tribes were Hussein and Sa'dun Shakir used to go hunting. After the revolution, Hussein had given these tribes many rifles. An announcement was put out on the radio to arrest Kazar and informed the nearest Ba'ath Party unit. Members of the tribe who became aware of this through the radio, so Kazar's caravan, surrounded it and detained him. Special operations helicopters were then dispatched to pick up Kazar and return him to Baghdad.

After Bakr obtained a clear picture of what had occurred, he started to cry, picked up his belongings and went from his palace to his residence. According to Hussein, Bakr said that he did not want to be the president. Bakr told Hussein he wanted Hussein to remain in the government so he could "slip out." Hussein claimed that he had made a similar statement to Bakr also about wanting to leave the government.

Following this, Hussein told people not to bother Bakr and to let him stay at home. Hussein then began arresting the alleged conspirators of this coup. He called Bakr to inform him that some of the conspirators were among the Ba'ath Party leadership. Hussein began organizing a meeting between himself, Bakr and leaders of the Ba'ath Party central and National Committees.

Hussein was asked how he knew that Kazar would be fleeing to Iran. He answered that when the announcement went out on the radio to look for Kazar, people started calling in sightings of him. Gradually, it was those periodic sightings that led him to believe that Kazar was heading towards Iran.

Hussein was asked if Kazar called Pres. Bakr, and he said, "No." Hussein said that apparently Kazar's vehicle had apparently become stuck in the mud. When he solicited the assistance of local farmers, they called for help. It was around this time that Kazar shot Ministers Shihab and Ghaydan. Shihab survived by pretending that he was dead.

Hussein was asked whether Kazar had called Pres. Bakr to negotiate the release of the hostages, and at the same time selected Abd Al-Khalig Al-Samarra'i's residence as a place to meet. Hussein denied this, stating that there was announcements on the emergency radio band that a coup had been attempted and that all Party members should meet at Abd Al-Khalig Al-Samarra'i's residence. Hussein did not know why this house was chosen as a meeting location, but suspected that the Party members were being called to one location to be arrested. When asked whether Samarra'i' was implicated in the coup simply because of the meeting, Hussein answered that a "committee" took care of this. Hussein does not remember who headed the "committee," including whether it was Izzat Ibrahim Al-Duri. Hussein stated, "I do not want to make a mistake on the details regarding something which I am not one hundred percent sure." Hussein acknowledged that Samarra'i' had been a Ba'ath member since 1968. When asked if Samarra'i 'spoke out on issues, Hussein said "the Ba'ath Party talk freely. This is only a media interpretation that people could not talk." Hussein stated that there are members of the Party still available, and he suggested that I talk with them. I asked Hussein if he was surprised by the allegations against Samarra'i'. He responded, "When we give someone in the Party something to do, we trust them. These and other things happen in a revolution."

Hussein then stated, "Whether I am the first person on the second person, all the questions come back to me. I am not afraid of taking responsibility in front of the wall or the people. You have to put blame not just on leadership, but also on the people who conspired such as Samarra'i'" Hussein added, "I want you to understand clearly about the situation. Yesterday, we talked about the fact that Nayif and Hardan were killed overseas. Ibrahim Daud was not killed. If the Iraqi government is being accused of all this, why did they not kill Daud?"

Hussein added, "As I recall, Bakr ruled until 1979 but was not called a dictator, but after I ruled, they called me a dictator." Hussein then asked, "After 1979, who was killed or assassinated inside or outside of a Iraq? Who was executed from the ministries or out of the leadership after 1979?"

Following these questions I said that these are unanswered questions which need to be clarified for the sake of history. Hussein said, "It's not enough to ask me you should ask other leaders. I advise you to talk to others." Hussein said he was not worried about answering questions.

I told Hussein that he was answering the questions for the same reasons they were being asked, for the sake of history. Hussein replied, "Sometimes, yes see me upset because some things are dark. During this period, we had good and bad times. We laughed and joked. Samarra'i' served, and we made jokes with him he made mistakes. We moved on. I hope you will be just, in what history you write.

I told Hussein "fortunately or unfortunately, I will have a major impact on your history." Hussein agreed and replied, "Nobody can say I have no bias. People think what they want. Everyone has his own opinions. People are not a computer. We all have flesh and blood."

Chapter 6

Ascendancy to Presidency

Beginning in 1973, Iraqi Pres. Bakr began having health problems including issues with his heart. Despite these problems, Bakr preformed his duties as best as he could. Periodically, Bakr told Hussein that he should retire and that he could no longer fulfill his duties as Pres. Hussein is unaware whether Bakr made such comments to others within the Ba'ath Party leadership. Hussein stated Bakr felt "close to Hussein."

Around this time, Hussein seriously considered leaving the government but remained in the Party. His main reason for wanting to leave the government was linked to the overthrow of the Ba'ath Party government 1963 Hussein believed this overthrow occurred because the Party leadership concentrated on the government and forgot about the Party. Hussein did not like the "power" and his position in the government. When he joined the revolution in 1968, his intention was not to stay in the government. Hussein had planned to stay involved only within the cells of the Party at the lower level. At that time, he believed it would be a "shame" to serve in the government. He likes the people and the Party, but believes it is difficult for the government to judge fairly. Hussein observed individuals he described as "kind and gentle" before serving in the government who subsequently became the opposite after their appointments to the government positions were finished. After the 1968 revolution, a governing Revolutionary command Council

(RCC) was formed. However, the announcement of the RCC was not made until one year later in 1969. The members of the RCC, with the exception of the military members, were not and "did not want to be known." For this reason, the announcement of the RCC was delayed. Hussein was "forced" to take a leadership position in the RCC. Party members asked Hussein whether he wanted the revolution to fail, implying it would without his participation, and that it was his responsibility to be a Party leader.

Hussein wanted Bakr to remain as president for as long as possible calming describing him as a "nice person." In 1979, however, Bakr contacted Hussein and asked him to meet in Bakr's office in the presidential palace. At this meeting, Bakr told Hussein he no longer wanted nor felt able to serve as president. Bakr implored Hussein to assume his duties, telling Hussein is he did not accept the "normal method" of appointment as president, he would use a radio to make an announcement that Hussein was now president. Hussein told Bakr that this means of announcing a successor would not be good for the country, the people, or the Party. Outsiders, or foreigners, especially would have thought something was wrong within Iraq. Thereafter, Tariq Aziz was asked to prepare an announcement regarding the change of leadership. A meeting of the RCC was convened in July, 1979. Hussein is unsure whether he or Bakr called the meeting.

At the meeting, Bakr explained to the RCC members that he wanted to step down since 1973. He further explained to the members that Hussein was ready to assume the presidency. Hussein described the meeting as being "like a family gathering." There were many emotions present including sadness. The transfer of the presidency to the same was conducted according to the Constitution. Hussein stated a vote was taken, but he does not remember whether it was by secret ballot or by raising hands. He was designated secretary general of the Party and Pres. of Iraq.

I asked him whether he observed any changes in himself upon assuming presidency, he responded, "no." He stated he became "stronger and closer to the people."

I asked Hussein what would he had done had he been allowed to leave the government, Hussein replied that he would have been a regular person, possibly a farmer. He would, however have continued as a Party member and continued attending meetings of the Party.

In my own personal opinion it would be difficult to imagine Hussein is a farmer. Hussein stated he was afraid to become a public figure. He stated that his situation changed as did his obligations, becoming almost personal. Hussein observed that while he served as president, thousands of people viewed themselves as being close to him. Until 1995, people did not elect him, rather Hussein stated, "The revolution brought me here." After 1995 and 2002, the people did, in fact vote for Anderlecht Hussein. After the elections, his relationship with the people became stronger, and Hussein now felt an obligation to those people who had voted for him. Hussein was not only obligated to the people by well, but also to the people "in front of the eyes of God."

I asked Hussein at the time of the meeting where Bakr announced his resignation, if the entire RCC supported him becoming president? Hussein responded there was nothing or no one against him to become the leader. Morally and out of respect for Bakr, some members asked the car to stay. The car, however, did not allow their wishes to influence is vital decision. Hussein viewed Bakr's decision is final because he, himself, could not convince Bakr to remain as president.

I did note reports which stated there was at least one outspoken person at the meeting who question Bakr's retirement and stated that Hussein's selection should be unanimous. Hussein stated this information is not correct. There was discussions about Bakr's resignation but not talk about the process for selecting Hussein. Others offered to assume some of the cars duties so that he might be able to remain as president. He did not accept these offers, however. At that time, Hussein was deputy secretary general of the Party and vice president of Iraq. As such, he was next in line to become president, a fact which could not have been questioned. Additionally, the Constitution specifically stated any selection of the president had to be made by a majority, not unanimous, vote. Some members talked about the possibility of postponing Bakr resignation. Hussein stated there are former RCC members still alive who can be questioned regarding this matter. I stated that some of the RCC members we have spoken to generally agree on the details provided by Hussein about this event. However some former RCC members also provided information indicating Mashhadi voiced his opinion to buy cars resignation and Hussein's selection as president at that referenced RCC meeting. Hussein replied that he had told me all the details known to him.

I stated a plot against Hussein was discovered shortly after he assumed the presidency. An infamous meeting took place on July 22, 1979 whereupon the details of the plot revealed to senior members of the Party. I added that the meeting was recorded on videotape, and viewed by me. Hussein stated that this matter was not a secret and the video was given to all Party members. Hussein does not remember whether the meeting was opened with comments by Taha Yasin Ramadan. He acknowledged that Mashhadi was brought before the assembly, admitted his participation in the plot against Hussein involving the Syrian government, and names some of the others who participated in the plot. Hussein's reaction and feelings were the same as anyone who had been betrayed by friends in the Party and the government, sadness and a feeling of being "back stabbed." This was especially true because the plot involved Arabs outside the government and the country. Hussein described these actions is treason and the participants as traders.

When Hussein became aware of the plot, he responded, "at the time." I pointed out that Mashhadi was arrested a few days before the meeting, approximately July 15, after Hussein became president. Hussein stated he became president on July 17. I responded that July 17 was the official date, although Hussein had actually assume the presidency almost one week prior.

I asked Saddam Hussein how the plot was discovered. Hussein asked, "Did you hear the video?" He added that the information on the video should be enough. I did note the video did not provide details about how the plot was discovered. Hussein responded, "These are secrets of the country." He emphasized that he still considered these detailed secrets despite the fact that the event occurred almost 25 years ago.

I've been steered the discussion to the video which was not a state secret. I told him the video depicted several present and future members of the senior leadership. Among those were Tariq Aziz and Ali Hasan Al-Majid, who was seen standing and shouting. The video names approximately 66 individuals as participants in the plot, including Adnan Hussein, Deputy Prime Minister, and Ghanim Abd Al-Jalil, Director of the Office of the President. Hussein stated

Adnan was the Minister of Planning and Secretary of the Committee for Oil and Agreements. Hussein acknowledge that Adnan may have already been appointed as Deputy Prime Minister after Hussein assume the presidency and before this meeting. Hussein acknowledged that a total of five RCC members, and none of the original 70 revolutionaries, were implicated in the plot. Hussein denied that any of the conspirators, including Adnan and Ghanim, were his friends. People who worked in the government were not his friends. Hussein stated that they were "not close to me." Like others, they were appointed to government positions. Some "made it" while some did not. When pointed out to Hussein that I saw him crying in the video when Ghanim's name was announced, Hussein responded that, as a human being, he still had feelings. As the head of his office, Hussein saw Ghanim every day delivering various papers. All of the members of the plot were in the leadership. Hussein remarked that treason makes you feel "sorrowful." When I noted that one might say Hussein had been betrayed by his closest colleagues, Hussein responded the most important thing is that they were in the government and they were with Hussein and the Party.

Hussein acknowledge that over 60 people were implicated, although not all were convicted. Hussein's further acknowledged that the names of the "conspirators" were announced by Mashhadi were read by Hussein from a list at the meeting. As a names were announced, the persons named were asked to stand up, and, one by one, was escorted from the hall by the Himaya.

Thereafter, a tribunal was held to adjudicate the matter and to decide punishment. Hussein stated he does not remember the exact number or activities of the persons who were found guilty and were executed or imprisoned, or who escaped, or who were found innocent and were released. He acknowledged that the entire matter, including executions, was concluded within approximately 16 days, or by August 8, 1979. Hussein believes the amount of time used during the process was "more than enough" for an unbiased and impartial trial. Although he believes this was enough time to be fair, Hussein acknowledged there might not have been adequate time to "go deep into things." When asked to clarify this statement, Hussein responded there may have been other conspirators who were not identified. Hussein does not know whether there were other participants, but he reiterated that the information available and that time utilized for the investigation were enough to convict those who were identified. He commented that the law says it is better for one guilty person to go free than for many innocent people to go to jail without being guilty.

Hussein stated he does not know the specific results of the investigation. This matter was decided by a court and the sentences were carried out thereafter. When questioned about Abd Al-Khaliq Al-Samarra'i's involvement and how it was possible for someone already imprisoned to be part of such a plot, Hussein responded, "Ask those who did the investigation." When asked to provide the names of the investigators, Hussein stated he does not remember. I noted that Barzan Al-Tikriti, having just been named Director of the Iraqi Intelligence Service (IIS), head of the investigation. Hussein replied that there must have been a committee, but he denied knowledge of the composition of any such committee. He further denied knowing anyone who might know the composition of this committee.

I asked about the involvement of the RCC in this investigation, Hussein first denied knowledge of any details. He observed that if the matter was decided by tribunal, there must have been an official committee. I reminded Hussein of a speech he gave on August 8,

1979, where and he stated that the RCC, formerly numbering 21, now included 16 members due to the implications of five RCC members in the plot. Hussein continued in the speech saying, of the 16 RCC members, three conducted the investigation and seven formed the tribunal which heard the facts and decide punishment. In the speech, Hussein added that this was the first time in the history of revolutionary movements and human struggle that over half of the supreme leadership of the nation took part in such a matter. Hussein responded to me, "good, very good." According to the Constitution, members of the RCC must be tried by other RCC members, not by a tribunal outside of the RCC. When question regarding the fairness or neutrality of the RCC conducting a trial of its own members, Hussein replied that fairness existed within the individuals of the RCC. The plot was not against them, it was against Hussein. Additionally, the Constitution, which dictates procedure, existed well before the plot.

I question regarding previous statements he made saying the plot was against the Party, Hussein replied, "I did not say that. I said it was against Saddam." The conspirators plotted with another country (Syria) to prevent Hussein from coming to power. While it is true Hussein was head of the Party, the plot was against him individually. Hussein believes there were individuals who did not want him in power because he would not be "easy to control." With another person as president, who had conspired with the five members of the RCC and the other country, others would have been able to control Iraq. Hussein acknowledged that a tentative agreement regarding unification of Syria and Iraq was being worked on at the time, specifically through Tariq Aziz. However, the plot ended that discussion/agreement as "anything based on plotting has no value." When questioned what other country hope to gain, Hussein responded, "ask them. We did not ask them."

47

Hussein denied any knowledge of a reward being paid to the individuals who discovered the plot. When question as to the reason for videotaping the meeting on July 22, Hussein stated the video was made in order to inform Party of what had occurred. He confirmed that, as seen in the video, there were many emotions present, including sadness. I pointed out that fear appeared to be the most notable motion, first from audience members, and then from those who were named and shouted their innocence upon being ordered to stand. Hussein acknowledged that he, himself, ordered at least one of the named individuals to leave the hall.

I noted three things in the video that seem to stand out, including Hussein smoking a cigar, the expression on Tariq Aziz' face, and Ali Hasan Al-Majid shouting about Al-Samarra'i and his belief that conspiracies would continue as long as Al-Samarra'i was alive. Hussein responded that he knows the meaning behind each example provided by me. He stated that he rarely smokes unless the "times are difficult." Hussein questioned the expression of Aziz, whether it was happy or sad one. I responded that he appeared to be scared. Hussein stated this "reading" by me was not correct, "we were all scared." But with regards to Ali Hasan, Hussein asked me whether I was implying Al-Samarra'i was executed simply because of the words of Ali Hasan.

Hussein stated copies of the video of the July 22, 1979 meeting were sent to Iraqi ambassadors and other countries. The videos were to be used by embassy officials to present information to Iraqis living outside of the country concerning events occurring within Iraq. Hussein denied knowledge of whether the video was shown to leaders of other countries. Hussein remarked, if it was shown to such persons, that would have been "a good thing, not a bad thing." Perhaps the video would have been shown to other leaders because another Arab country was involved in the plot. Regarding whether the video was made and distributed to demonstrate that Hussein was in charge of Iraq, Hussein responded that I had seen the video and "this is your opinion, you have that right."

I provided comments reportedly made by Hussein around the time of the plot wherein he said, "With our Party methods, there is no chance for anyone who disagrees with us to jump on a couple of tanks and overthrow us." Hussein stated he does not remember making such a comment, but believes he could explain that these words were part of his thinking. This message was directed not only at the other country with whom the conspirators were plotting but also to all Party members.

I asked Hussein about his sincerity of his reported previous statement to Bakr in the 1960s and 1970s wherein he expressed a desire to leave the government. Hussein responded by saying that after 1974, he believed that he had a moral obligation to the Iraqi people. After many discussions with Pres. Bakr, Hussein acknowledged it was "his fate." From this time forward, he decided he would accept such an appointment and plan for the presidency.

Chapter 7

Sa'dun Shakir

Pres. Hussein was informed the session would be a continuation of previous discussions. Topics to be covered would include a discussion of Sa'dun Shakir, among others.

Hussein acknowledged that Shakir was an example of someone in the Ba'ath Party (the Party) who had "served out his abilities." Nevertheless, Shakir with someone with whom Hussein maintained contact after his departure from service to the Party.

Hussein first met Shakir in the Taji prison near Baghdad. Both Hussein and Shakir had been sentenced to prison upon change of the Iraqi government in late 1963 when a coup led by Adb Al-Salem Aref overthrew the Ba'ath Party government. During 1965 or 1966, Hussein and Shakir were transferred to Prison #1 also near Baghdad. At some point, check here was released but continued visiting Hussein in prison. During this time, their friendship continued and developed more. Eventually Hussein and Adb AL-Karim Al-Shaykhil escaped from prison with the assistance of Shakir, who served as their driver during the escape.

After escaping from prison, Shakir was still a member of the Party and served in that capacity. During this period, Hussein continued friendly relations with him. He described Shakir as a very trusted person who Hussein considered as a friend to him and to his children. Secure was one of the original 70 "revolutionaries" of 1968.

I asked the question regarding positions held in the Party by Shakira, Hussein commented that, like any other leader, Shakir what accept any assignment. Hussein does not remember any of these assignments and stated this was not important. He was a friend and that was what is important. Hussein suggested that I should ask Shakir here in order to confirm this information.

I asked if Shakir was the Director of the Iraqi Intelligence Service (IIS), Hussein replied it is well – known that he was the IIS director. I opinion that it is a generally accepted that someone in charge of an organization such as an intelligence service should have certain qualifications and abilities prior to appointment to such a position. Hussein replied, "We were all young revolutionaries." As such, they did not have the necessary experience and learned "on the job." Hussein added that regarding management matters, they learned from the Party. Hussein stated meeting people is the most difficult thing in life. Whoever can meet people in the Party and the masses, will be effective in their jobs. Hussein continued saying Party members "gave it a try" with some succeeding and some failing. Party members continued in their position until the responsibilities of their work overcame individual abilities. At this point, they were replaced regarding Party members with a military background, Hussein noted this military experience was limited and did not necessarily translate into something useful for government affairs.

Hussein acknowledge Shakir served as IIS director at an important time of the revolution. He noted, however that the entire history of the revolution is important. Perhaps, Shakir did not serve at the most critical time. Hussein added, "Difficulties became larger when the job becomes larger." I then turned the discussion to Shaykhil Hussein acknowledged Shaykhil was a fellow revolutionary and a friend. Hussein and shake at hand participated in the assassination

51

attempt against Iraqi president Qassem in 1959. Each escape Iraq and fled to down Damascus, Syria. They are, Hussein and Shaykhil's friendship and brotherhood continued to grow stronger. After Syria, their friendship continued upon moving to Cairo together.

After the first Ba'ath Party of 1963, Hussein and Shaykhli went "underground" together. They remained "underground" until the July, 1968 revolution in Iraq and the resumption of power by the Ba'ath Party. Thereafter, Hussein and Shaykhli served in the Party leadership together until 1971.

Hussein commented that Shaykhli had a very good mind but did not concentrate and focus on the job at hand. According to Hussein, Shaykhli like to "live and entertain himself." Hussein told Shaykhli help the Party perceived him. Later, the majority of Party leadership voted to remove Shaykhli from his position. He was later murdered in Baghdad in 1980.

I pointed out that Hussein had omitted some details of his relationship with Shaykhli including the fact that the two of them had served in prison at the same time after the 1963 overthrow of the Ba'ath Party government becoming friends. As is commonly understood, I also noted Shaykhli once saved Hussein's life. Hussein responded, "In what sense?" I then relayed the details of an incident during the "underground" years of the Ba'ath Party between 1963 in 1968. According to the story, Hussein was at Shaykhli's apartment late one night. Hussein decided to leave the apartment and spend the night at a location where weapons for the Party were stored. However, Shaykhli convinced Hussein to remain at his place. Later that same night, the weapons storage location was aided by the police. Some believe Hussein might have been killed, or at a minimum, arrested if he had been at the location.

Hussein acknowledged this story is true and that he was with Shaykhli at this time. However, he stated the police could not have captured or killed him. Shaykhli driving, Hussein went to the weapons location the next morning. Upon arrival, a policeman at the location put the barrel of his machine gun in Hussein's face as he rang the bell of the house. Simultaneously, Shaykhli sped away from the location in the car. Hussein explained that although Shaykhli was a brave man, people react differently in different situations.

At this time, Hussein was not widely known and was someone who would not have been recognized. As such, the policeman did not recognize him. Hussein pretended not to know anything and ask whether this was "Mohammed's" residence. Hussein was not concerned about being shot or killed as the police in Iraq do not kill someone easily, unless their life is seriously threatened. Additionally, people in Iraq generally "know each other" and there are many tribal influences. Even if the law permits such conduct, tribes will seek revenge. Hussein continued his story saying he surprised the policeman by pushing his machine gun aside and pulling a pistol which he (Hussein) had concealed under his shirt. Hussein ordered the policeman to place his hands on Hussein's car, which had been previously left at the location and was likely the reason the house was discovered. Hussein did not want to kill the officer, but decided to fire around in the air over the policeman said. The gun malfunctioned, however, Hussein "reloaded." He told the policeman he would fire one round over his head, and if he moved, a second round into his body. He then fired the round over the policeman's head and the officer "became like a dog." A standoff then occurred as some of Hussein's "comrades" had been arrested

53

by the police inside the house. These "comrades" heard all the activity outside and told the police their comrade Saddam had arrived with a big group and would kill the policeman. Simultaneously, one of the men in the car with Shaykhli returned to the house with the machine gun. The police then acquiesced to the "comrades" in the house asking them for their help and to be saved from Hussein and his men. Thereafter, the standoff ended without bloodshed. Hussein ended this portion of his discussion saying there are many stories from the "underground"., All of them like "scenes in the movie's."

Hussein was told that Shaykhli was described, similar to Hussein, as a prominent and popular Party member at that time. Hussein responded there is no need and it is not important to compare one person to another. Each person is different, one is not better than the other.

Hussein also acknowledged Shaykhil served as Foreign Minister until 1971, whereupon he was removed from his position by the leadership. Hussein stated that removal of any individual from a position requires a decision by the leadership. Not all may agree on the removal, but a majority was required. In Hussein's opinion, Shaykhli could have continued his service to the Party and the government. At that time, Hussein believes securely could have been "criticized" and given the chance to correct his behavior. Shaykhli would never have been elected as a Party member without the support of Hussein. Because if Shaykhli's lack of concentration on his work and failure to accept criticism, the Party leadership was "not convinced" of him and decided on his removal.

I asked if Shaykhli was viewed as a potential successor to Pres. Bakr, Hussein did not agree and said this statement was too strong.

Hussein commented that it appeared as if I was implying that he removed those from leadership viewed as threats to Hussein's position of leadership. From the underground days, Hussein was already in charge. While in prison, the Ba'ath Party leadership sent a letter notifying Hussein of their recommendation that you become a member of the Ba'ath Party Central committee. Hussein answered the letter, "What good am I in a prison?" He asked the Party to find someone else, however, they did not listen to his opinion. Thereafter, the car and Hussein service to members of the Central committee, a body considered above the regional committee and all other Party components. The car served as Sec. General and Hussein served as deputy Sec. General while "underground."

Hussein commented that it is embarrassing to talk about one's own positions. His status in the Party was known, and even before the revolution. All those appointed to Party positions, dead or alive today, deserve these appointments. Basically, it came down to who was elected. Hussein stated, "It is difficult to talk about myself." Within the Party, members do not like to talk about themselves. Hussein had recommended that members not talk about themselves.

I pointed out that it is commonly believed, both inside and outside Iraq, that Hussein's potential rivals in the Party were eliminated during the period between the 1968 revolution and Hussein's ascendancy to the presidency in 1979. Hussein denied that those on the inside of Iraq would say or believe such information he agreed that the information could've come outside Iraq according to Hussein, this conclusion is the opinion of these people and not necessarily a fact.

Regardless of the information, Hussein stated any examination of this idea needs to be conducted logically. Hussein stated there are many examples in history throughout the world of similar ascension to power after a revolution. In Egypt, Nasser and Sadat were the only individuals who "state" with the revolution, with Nasser eventually becoming leader of the country. In France, a single soldier, Napoleon, became the leader of the country after the French Revolution when others gave up. American history is also full of examples of this phenomenon. In Hussein's opinion, these are the "revolutionary ways."

According to Hussein, previous uprisings, such as the French Revolution, were tragedies when compared to the times in which we live in now. Revolutions are a new step in government, not a "liberal way" where someone is chosen and groom to be a leader. Revolutions come from the people.

The 1968 revolution in Iraq included 70 "revolutionaries." Very few of them continuing government and/or Party service after the revolution. Some were appointed to positions and performed well, some did not. All of them did not have the ability to lead and be professional. Some continued in service while others dropped out over time. Hussein stated that all were servants of the people.

When questioned whether he believed Nasser became a dictator, Hussein replied that he did not agree. Upon responding to a request from me to define dictatorship, Hussein stated this is a form of government where one person rolls alone, without a parliament, counsel, or committee. Hussein did not agree with the characterization that Nasser's government fit this definition. Hussein stated Nasser had a parliament. However, a parliament is not possible at the beginning of a revolution. Normally, a Revolutionary Council is first established and is later followed by a parliament or People's committee. Hussein does not like comparing

Iraq and is 1968 revolution to Nasser and Egypt. Nasser was a military person who did not have a political Party. In Iraq, the Ba'ath had a Party ranging from the cells in villages all the way to the leadership as well as a parliament elected by the people. The leadership of the Party and the Revolutionary Command Council (RCC) discuss everything.

I asked him whether Hussein and Shaykhli remained friends after Shaykhli's departure from the Party service, Hussein stated his friends were among those with whom he met regularly in the leadership. He did not have any friends outside of the Party and the leadership. A true friend has "obligations." Hussein considered Shakir as the person closest to him after the 1968 revolution. Whenever Hussein needed to discuss something, he would send for Shakir and they would have lunch together and talk. After Shakir left government service, Hussein did not remember how many times they met. Hussein stated Shaykhli "kept up good relations" with his sons Qusay and Uday. I asked about securely end of period of time after his departure from the government service, Hussein stated his feelings of friendship remain the same, but the two did not spend the same amount of time together. Due to the demands of work, Hussein did not have time to associate with those outside of work, the Party, or the leadership.

I asked if he had special feelings about Shaykhli, who was shot and killed in Baghdad in 1980, Hussein stated, "yes." I asked if she killers were captured, Hussein responded, "I don't think so." An investigation took place, but the crime was not solved. Hussein stated that not all crimes committed are ultimately sold. He added that other crimes, including those committed against his cousins and those involving the deaths of various Iraqi dignitaries and ministers, remained unsolved. Hussein noted that not all crimes are solved elsewhere in the world, such as in America, France, or Italy. When questioned whether it was usual for a crime involving the murder of a foreign government minister, a former revolutionary, and a former friend of the Pres. of Iraq to go unsolved, Hussein reported, "what do you want to say. Why are you going around the subject?" There are others who are close to Hussein in the leadership who were targets of assassination attempts, including Tariq Aziz, Uday Hussein, and others. These crimes remain unsolved as well. It happens in Iraq, just as it happens elsewhere in the world. Hussein acknowledged the possibility that some people may say Shaykhli was killed by the Iraqi government. He added that some people might say anything. Logically, those who say this are probably the same people who say Shaykhli could have become President.

Chapter 8

Events Leading to the Invasion of Kuwait

Hussein stated that after the war in Iran from 1980 – 1988, Iraqi is trying to rebuild. Hussein likened the situation with Kuwait as similar to win two individuals fight, the fight ends, and the two parties go their separate ways. Thereafter, one of the previous disputing parties is bothered by someone else who also wants to fight. Then, there is no choice but to fight again

According to the saying, Khomeini and Iran would have occupied all of the Arab world if it had not been for Iraq. As such, Iraq expected the Arab world to support them during and after the war. However, Iraq saw the opposite regarding support, especially from Kuwait. At the end of the war as Iraq began the rebuilding process, the price of oil was approximately $7 per barrel. In Hussein's opinion, Iraq could not possibly rebuild its infrastructure and economy with oil prices at that level. Kuwait was especially at fault regarding these low prices.

In an effort to solve the situation and stimulate economic recovery, Iraqi descent Dr. Hammadi, Iraqi Minister of Foreign Affairs, to Kuwait. Hammadi, and the Iraqi leadership's conclusion after the meeting was that the oil price situation was not just a responsibility/work of the Kuwaitis. Iraq believed some other entity, some larger power was behind this "conspiracy."

Iraq also sent government officials to Saudi Arabia to convince the Saudis to pressure Kuwait. In addition, the Saudi minister of oil came to Iraq and held talks about oil prices, the Iraqi economy, and the actions of Kuwait. Hussein claimed that the Kuwaiti official said, "will make the economy in Iraq be so bad, one would be able to sleep with an Iraqi woman for 10 dinars." Hussein told the Saudis that if Kuwait did not stop interfering in Iraqi affairs, he would make the Kuwaiti dinar worth 10 fils.

Hussein stated that when Kuwait was faced with the facts regarding "stealing" Iraqi oil using the practice of slant drilling, they admitted to having taken "only 2 ½ billion barrels." They said this fact as if it was not significant.

I asked how he regarded the problems with Kuwait, Hussein stated that Iraqi sent delegates to other Gulf countries which Hussein does not remember. These delegates explained the Kuwaiti situation and the Iraqi situation. The other countries promise to correct oil prices at the next meeting of the organization of petroleum exporting countries (OPEC).

At the next OPEC meeting, a decision was made to fix the oil price at $16 – $17 per barrel, as remembered by Hussein. Kuwait concurred with this decision. Thereafter, the Kuwaiti Minister of Oil or Minister of Foreign Affairs stated Kuwait would not abide by the OPEC decision.

I asked about loan debts owed to Gulf countries as a result of support received during the Iran Iraq war, Hussein stated these were not loans and were supposed to be free aid from these countries the countries had originally use the word loan as a formality only to disguise am the purpose of the funds from Iran. When Iraq was

60

informed the money was actually from loans, Iraqi held discussions with these countries, including Kuwait, in order to resolve these debts. Because the money had been "registered as loans" to Iraq could not secured loans from other countries in order to rebuild.

Hussein stated that twice he discussed a change in oil prices to $25 per barrel. Once, when the price per barrel reached $50, Hussein dictated a letter to Tariq Aziz, which was sent to be Thoura Newspaper. In the letter, he told the oil producing countries that they should not take advantage of the industrialized nations. Hussein asked them to reduce the price per barrel to $25. He commented that this was strange at the time as a Iraq had oil and could use the money. When the prices drop to seven dollars per barrel in 1989 – 90, Hussein called for an increase to $24 – $25 per barrel. In Hussein's opinion, this price would not burden the customer or hurt the producer.

I asked Hussein what kind of message that he did receive by Kuwait's action or lack of action with regards to Iraq, Hussein stated "this confirmed our information" that there was a "conspiracy" against Iraq, the Iraqi leadership, and the Iraqi's economy. And Hussein's opinion, the visit of US Gen. Schwarzkopf to Kuwait also provided further confirmation. His visit included "sand planning" or wartime preparations for the invasion of Iraq confirming what Hussein and the leadership already believe. Previous to this event, Kuwait's relationship with the United States and Great Britain was well known. When noted to Hussein that the United States military visits many countries throughout the world conducting exercises which are not indicators of a "conspiracy", Hussein asked," and what other country does work scoffed do "sand planning" like Kuwait?" Hussein further question which other countries Schwarzkopf conducted negotiations with in order to enter for defensive purposes. Hussein acknowledged that he understands the existence and nature of exercises conducted by the United States in Egypt and Jordan. However, when exercises are planning casts Iraqi as an enemy and includes ways to defend Kuwait or attack Iraq, this is a different situation than other exercises.

Hussein discuss the perception in the West regarding Iraq in the months leading up to the war in Kuwait. After Iraq's defeat of Iran, the media discussed Iraq as a military threat to the region. Iraqi, however, was not "within Soviet circles" and was attempting to rebuild its economy. Iraqi was also starting to build its relations with United States.

So, the United States made Iraq its enemy through three means or for three reasons. First, the "Zionist" power and influence in the United States dictates form policy. Any country viewed as a threat to Israel, such as Iraq becomes a target of a "conspiracy." Hussein offered proof of this position stating Israel issued an official statement saying that any peace agreement with Arab countries must include Iraq. Hussein claims Israel is not hoping for peace only that other countries abide by their wishes. Israel used its influence over the West against Nasser in Egypt similar to his positions vis-à-vis Iraq. This "Zionist" influence extends throughout the United States to include elections. Secondly, there are formerly two superpowers in the world, the United States and the Soviet Union. According to Hussein, the world's existence then was "better than now" as it was easier for two powers to agree rather than attempt to get many to agree. Each of the two superpowers attempts to get other countries to side with them, forging a balance of power in the world. With the collapse of this balance, however, the United States was that the loan as the sole superpower. The United States is now viewed as attempting to dictate its will to the rest of the world including Iraq.

When countries do not agree with the United States, such as Iraq, they become enemies. The third reason the United States made Iraq its enemy is for economic purposes. Certain entities within the United States, including weapons manufacturers and elements in the military, favorable award due to financial profit which can be raped. This is true for the company selling everything from carpets to tanks in support of a war. Hussein added that America discovered the war in Afghanistan was not enough to sustain the profit making of the military – industrial complex of America. Thus, the war began with Iraq. After the collapse of the Soviet Union, all of these internal and neck stood a reasons combined to compel the United States to make Iraq its enemy.

Prior to the invasion of Kuwait, Hussein stated that there was a meeting of the Iraqi Revolutionary Command Council (RCC) in which a discussion of the matter took place. The Iraqi leadership of the RCC had hoped the Saudis would "interfere" and have a solution. The deputy chairman of the RCC had traveled to Saudi Arabia to solicit their assistance but returned without success. Thereafter, the matter could only be discussed and decided upon in favor of military action. Hussein acknowledge the possibility that one or more RCC members opposed or voted against the invasion, but he does not specifically remember any such opposition. He does not remember if the majority or all of the RCC members agreed on military action. Hussein stated, "I was against attacking if a solution could be found." The last attempt at reaching a solution occurred during the previously referenced visit to Saudi Arabia in which the deputy chairman of the RCC met with the brother of Kuwaiti leader Sheikh Sabah. The final decision to invade Kuwait was made in order to "defend by attacking." Hussein further justified the invasion based upon historical facts. He stated that history dictates Kuwait is part of Iraq.

Hussein stated the objective of the invasion was "the one announced." That is, Kuwaitis were to rule themselves and would decide what kind of relations they would have with Iraq. As for the Kuwaiti leaders, Hussein stated that they were "conspiratorial" against Iraq, Kuwait, and all Arab countries. These leaders conspiring even after they left Kuwait upon the invasion by Iraq. They were controlled by the United States.

Because of the countries "conspiracy" with the United States, Kuwait did not expect the "blow to them." Hussein stated Kuwait deserved "10 blows." Kuwait was not as strong militarily as Iran. Kuwait's lack of defensive positions is not indicate of the absence of plans with the United States. The plan was discussed during the previously referenced "sand planning" may have been offensive in nature, not defense of. The reasons for Iraq's invasion existed, with or without the presence of American forces. As they did in the most recent war, the United States "created" the reasons to fight Iraq in Kuwait in 1991. Hussein denied creating this "conspiracy" as a justification for the invasion of Kuwait. He claimed documents discovered by Iraq in Kuwait prove the existence of the Kuwaiti "conspiracy" with the United States.

Hussein remarked, "we can discuss this for days." The United States and 28 other countries took seven months to mobilize forces for the war in 1991. This mobilization occurred because of the power of Iraq and the perceived military threat it posed. This threat motivated US politicians to support action against Iraq. In addition, the financial interests of the companies that could profit from a war also motivated support for action against Iraq. The preemptive strike by Iraq into Kuwait was conducted so that defensive lines could not be completed. Hussein reiterated the lack of American forces in Kuwait does not mean there was not a "conspiracy."

Hussein restated that the goal of the invasion of Kuwait was to allow Kuwaitis the right to "beside the way they wanted to deal with Iraq." Hussein denied that the declarations of Kuwait as the 19th province of Iraq contradicts his previous statement. According to Hussein, a Kuwaiti government was established after the invasion and included a prime minister and various other ministers. Hussein denied that Iraq E RCC member Ali Hasan Al-Majid was appointed Governor of Kuwait. He added that the Kuwaiti cabinet decided to "join the Iraqis." When questioned whether the Kuwaitis were given a choice, Hussein asked whether Iraqi's were given a choice to vote their opinion regarding the recent war in Iraq. He continued that Iraq's acts with respect to Kuwait where more logical than the United States position on Iraq in the most recent war. Hussein stated the designation of Kuwait as a 19th province was "deserved and logical." In 1961 or 1962, then Iraqi Pres. Qassem wanted to make Kuwait a district of Iraq.

Hussein emphasize that he has already explained why no other actions were taken to avoid the invasion as well as the reasons Kuwait was designated the 19th province. The political solutions for this matter were completely removed when America attacked. Hussein claimed Iraq "would have gone the other way" if the United States had not attacked them. With political solutions exhausted, two options remain. Iraq could have withdrawn from Kuwait, with attacks against their forces not likely to stop during the withdrawal. Iraq would have been "laughingstock" of the world. Iraq he forces would have been especially reluctant to fight if Kuwait had not been declared as the 19th province. The other solution, and the appropriate one, was not to withdrawal and to declare Kuwait as the 19th province so be Iraqi forces would fight with greater vigor.

Chapter 9

Invasion of Kuwait Continued

Hussein stated that he devised a plan for the Iraqi invasion of Kuwait. Because the geography of Kuwait is essentially open land, neither specific tactical planning nor special assets were needed to affect this operation. Any person with basic military knowledge could have put together an effective invasion plan.

The invasion of Kuwait was accomplished within 2 ½ hours, equivalent to that previously estimated. Hussein stated it should have taken no more than one hour. He believes it should have occurred more quickly than originally estimated due to support for the invasion from the Kuwaiti people. Hussein reiterated a previous statement to me that Iraqi was asked by the Kuwaiti people to invade their country in order to remove the Kuwaiti leadership. When asked to clarify how the Kuwaiti citizens communicated their desires to the Iraqi government prior to the invasion, Hussein stated some, not all, Kuwaitis felt this way. He added, "We felt they were asking."

Hussein was asked about the assault on the coastal city of Khafji and who designed this attack, Hussein stated, "Me." He added that he would not shift the blame to any of his friends. Hussein stated that military planning was easy after eight years of war with Iran from 1980 to 1988. Any military operation requires knowledge of the geography of the area and knowledge of the weapons and the capabilities of the enemy as well as one's own capabilities. Other important factors include the training, logistical support, and morale of the troops. With such knowledge, the military operations against Khafji was simple to plan. The land was opened, similar to southern Iraq, and provided no "complications." The only concern was enemy air power capability.

I questioned whether the purpose of the assault on Khafji was to force the coalition forces into a groundwork, Hussein replied that military experts knew that any ground attack against the Iraqi army was a difficult task. His opinion that 2 million troops would have been needed to fight the Iraqi ground forces. Aircraft, however, could be used to strike Iraqi forces and thereafter returned to base. The preliminary information available to Iraq indicated that coalition ground forces were in the vicinity of Khafji. For this reason, Iraqi forces decided to attack the location and to "force a fight." Hussein stated that it seemed that coalition forces withdrew upon attack by Iraqi forces. Thereafter, Iraqi ground forces remained in the area. As time passed, erect lost soldiers, ammunition, and equipment. Many Iraqi soldiers died as a result of repeated coalition air assaults without ever see in the enemy approaching overland.

Hussein denied that Iraqi forces were defeated at Khafji, forcing them to withdrawal. Hussein stated Iraqi did not intend to occupy the city. Iraqi ground forces went to the location to fight with coalition ground forces. Upon encountering little to no ground resistance, Iraqi forces withdrew on the second day, of their own choosing. Hussein noted that it seemed coalition forces were not aware of the Iraqi withdrawal for a few days. Hussein acknowledge that coalition forces had air supremacy.

I asked if he was trying to capture American prisoners of war (POWs) as an objective for the assault on Khafji. Hassan stated one of the principles of war is to kill or capture the enemy. After 14 days of coalition bombardment of Iraq he forces, Iraqi wanted to force casualties upon coalition forces. However, erect preferred to capture coalition personnel. In Hussein's opinion, there would have had a "lot of the fact" on the enemy. Hussein acknowledge that the assault on Khafji may not have been effective and may have shown coalition forces Iraqs strengths. This may have led to prolonged coalition airstrikes and a delay in the ground war.

Hussein believes Iraqi forces should have conducted their ground assault even earlier. The operation was delayed an additional week, creating an opportunity for the coalition to conduct additional airstrikes which weakened the Iraqi ground forces. Hussein denied that there was a plan to capture American POWs as a method of trying to prevent continued coalition air attacks.

Hussein stated that he, and no one else in the Iraqi government or leadership, gave the orders to fire SCUD missiles at Israel. He stated, "Everything that happened to us was because of Israel." Hussein added that all the "bad things" for Arabs came as a result of Israel's actions. He's dated that Israel first attack Iraq in 1981 destroying the country's only nuclear reactor. As far as Iraq was concerned, the war with Israel was "still on." During this conflict in 1991, Hussein reason that the United States would stop the war if Israel was "hurt." He also wanted to punish the country that he considered as the source of all the problems. Hussein denied that one of his reasons for striking Israel was SCUD missiles was to cause is really retaliation, a collapse of the coalition, and withdrawal of Arab support for the coalition. According to Hussein, the Arab countries which supported the coalition have been "shamed." Thus, any withdrawal of their support against Iraq was inconsequential.

Hussein stated there were two reasons for the war in 1991, loyal and Israel. He added that Kuwait would not have considered doing anything against Iraq unless "pushed" by another country (the United States). When I pointed out to Hussein that historians believe Iraq acted first, Hussein replied that this was the result (of Kuwait's actions) and not the reasons (for the war).

Hussein denied that Iraqi forces withdrew from Kuwait following their defeat. He insisted Iraqi forces withdrew as the result of an official proclamation. This cease-fire, including the Iraqi withdrawal, was negotiated by the Russians and accepted by Iraq. Coalition air attacks against Iraqi ground forces occurred while troops were retreating under official orders from the Iraqi leadership. Hussein denied that Iraqi forces would have been eliminated if they had not withdrawal.

Hussein stated an Iraqi plan of withdrawal existed as early as August 12, 1990 however Iraq found no government and the international community nor in the Arab world which would agree to negotiate the terms of this plan. The president of France expressed support for the plan, but subsequently withdrew the support after receiving pressure from the United States. Thereafter, Iraqi accepted the previously discussed Russian initiative. Hussein denied that the plan was accepted because of huge Iraqi military losses.

I then turned the discussion of the letter dated February 19, 1991 from Hussein Kamil, in the name of Iraqi Pres. Hussein to Ali Hassan Al-Majid. The letter stated, in part, that the Iraqi military should remove any and all property from Kuwait which will aid in the rebuilding of Iraq. Hussein stated the normal method of conveying directions from the president would be via letters from the Presidential Diwan. Kamil was not a secretary, but was simply one of the Iraqi ministers. Kamil was "known for his way of doing things." Upon being read the letter by the translator, Hussein asked whether the document referred to items used by the Iraqi military in Kuwait or the things from Kuwait itself. He added that he'd never instructed the Iraqi military to remove items, either their own equipment or Kuwaiti items. Hussein opinion that the letter may refer to equipment in Kuwait that was utilized by the various Iraqi ministers for critical services such as electricity, water, transportation, and telephone service. He stated the letter was dated nine days before the cease-fire. Hussein denied that the letter referred to Kuwaiti property. He stated it was simply a letter from one minister's subordinate to another minister, asking for the return of material taken to Kuwait by Iraqi forces. Hussein stated that he did not issue the letter. He asked what items or materials were taken from Kuwait after this letter was published.

I asked whether members of the Iraqi leadership were allowed to issue letters in the name of the president without his knowledge, Hussein stated, "there had been bad elements everywhere. The (Hussein Kamil) is dead now." Hussein denied knowledge of whether the other members of the Iraqi leadership acted on authority of the president without actually having power delegated to them by Hussein. Hussein acknowledged that the reference letter was not conveyed in an official manner. He reiterated that the official method of issuance of such a letter, upon orders from Hussein, would have been to send a communication from the presidential Diwan to Ali Hassan Al-Majid, in this case. This letter would have specifically enumerated the powers to be delegated to the particular individual, in this case, Hussein Kamil.

The Kuwaiti government indicated that the Iraqi invasion and occupation of Kuwait cost $180 billion in damages to the country,

Hussein asked for the source of this information. When told the source was Kuwait, Hussein asked which neutral or legal entity question Kuwait regarding the basis of their conclusion. His opinion was "no one" asked Kuwait for the details of their investigation of this matter. Hussein again questioned the existence of evidence supporting these Kuwaiti assertions.

Hussein reiterated information provided in a previous interview stating, "Kuwait is Iraqi." According to Hussein, Kuwait was "stolen" from Iraq by a British resolution. He added that if Kuwait had not been a country with oil, it would have not have been "stolen." Hussein stated that the arrogance of the Kuwaiti rulers made them "stupid" and ignited the war. He further stated that he understands that the United States, located across the Atlantic Ocean, would want Iraq to be poor. However, he cannot understand how Kuwait would want to exist next to a "hungry country."

Hussein emphasize that he is not saying that Kuwait did not have the right to make these statements. He again questioned the identity of the neutral entity which examined this matter and whether it was discussed with Iraq. Hussein suggested that something similar to a court should have been formed to hear the details from both sides and to decide this matter. However this did not happen.

Hussein stated that just prior to the latest war, American officials said all Iraqi debts would be forgiven including monies owed to Kuwait. And Hussein's opinion, this proved any amount reportedly owed to Kuwait was not a legal debt and was a "political" matter. He added that this policy was driven by the United States and not the United Nations (UN), Kuwait, or any other entity.

I told Hussein that Kuwait never ask for compensation for the damages suffered during the Iraqi invasion and occupation. Kuwait did however asked for the return of 605 prisoners of war (POWs). To date, these POWs have not been returned. Hussein stated these Kuwaiti's were not "captives" and are missing as characterized by the UN resolution. He stated that "many stories and novels have been woven" around this issue, similar to the matter of Iraqi weapons of mass destruction (WMD). The Kuwaiti POW accusation have been proven to be false, however, similar to the WMD rumors. Hussein stated that individuals often become "missing" during a war. He provided as examples the one coalition individual still missing from the first Gulf War and the thousands of Iraqis and Iranians missing from the war between the two countries. As for the 605 Kuwaitis, Hussein stated that Kuwait knows their fate. Hussein denied knowledge that 605 Kuwaitis were captured in circumstances other than combat after the Iraqi invasion of Kuwait.

Hussein acknowledge that Aziz Saleh Al-Numan was governor of Kuwait during the Iraqi occupation. As such, he reported directly to the Iraqi minister of interior, a position held by Ali Hassan al-Majid at the time. Al-Numan was appointed by him or by decree of the Revolutionary command Council (RCC). In Iraq, the Constitution sets forth the authority of the RCC and the president who is also the chairman of the RCC. Some governmental appointments such as those given to high-ranking officials in the military, judges, and general directors are based on a "Republican" directive. Hussein explained that the Iraqi system does not prevent the president from submitting a name for consideration for appointment and requesting subsequent feedback from the RCC. Decisions in Iraq are signed by the president. It is his prerogative to consult or not to consult anyone. Hussein stated "his style" was to always consult with others when the time came to make a decision. Governors were assigned based

72

on a "Republican" or presidential directive. Hussein does not remember if he discussed the appointment with Al-Numan with the RCC.

I question him in regards to Iraq using Kuwaitis, Japanese, and Westerners as human shields during the first Gulf War including the positions of them at key sites such as communication centers and military positions, Hussein denied that such individuals were taken to Iraqi military positions. He added that Iraqi government did not, however, prevent individuals from voluntariness human shields to protect facilities such as communication centers. I question whether such volunteers existed in 1991, Hussein replied, "I do not remember."

The translator read to Hussein and Iraqi government communication from Qusay Hussein concerning the usage of Kuwaiti prisoners as human shields. Hussein stated that he has no information about this letter. When noted to Hussein that the document was recovered by American forces from an Iraqi government building and was deemed legitimate, Hussein stated, "I have answered." He asked whether the captives discussed in this communication were ever questioned about being held in the Iraqi captivity are being used as human shields. Hussein stated that Iraq released all the Kuwaiti captives. Upon being told the document was dated March 14, 2003, Hussein stated, "it is a forgery. It is impossible." He suggested that the communication should be examined closely to determine authenticity and that he had thought it was dated 1991. Hussein stated that if the date of the document is 2003, it is a forgery. He added that Iraq did not have captives at that time. Hussein stated that Qusay was not the type of person to "make up things." He reiterated that experts in the United States and in Iraq should scrutinize this document for authenticity.

I questioned him about chemical weapons and why Iraq did not use them in the first Gulf War. Hussein replied that he had been asked this question previously and had answered. When noted to him that I had not previously asked this question, Hussein replied that he believed it was strange that I or anyone else what asked this question, not just at this point but at any time. He stated that it is not Iraqi policy to use chemical weapons against coalition forces. Hussein commented that this was a discussion of history, not unrealistic hypotheticals. He asked how Iraq would have been described if it had use chemical weapons. Hussein replied to his own question, "We would have been called stupid." According to the saying chemical weapons, and their use, were never discussed by Iraqi officials before or during the 1991 war.

As stated during a previous interview, Hussein acknowledged a meeting in January 1991 just before the war with US Secretary of State James Baker and Iraqi Foreign Minister Tariq Aziz. Hussein remembers a statement by Baker to "Take Iraq back to the preindustrial age." He stated that Iraq would not be intimidated by threats, however, especially when coming from someone in "a strong position." Hussein denied knowledge that part of this discussion concerned the position of the United States regarding Iraq's possible use of chemical weapons should hostilities occur. According to Hussein, "we decided the right thing to do." He stated that the use of chemical weapons did not "cross our minds."

Hussein stated that Sultan Hashem, Iraqi Ministry of Defense, and Saleh, Second Corps Commander, represented Iraq at eight cease-fire talks during the first Gulf War. There positions and viewpoints were the same as those of the Iraqi leadership, to secure a cease-fire and to start the withdrawal of foreign forces from Iraq. Hussein stated Iraq had no goal of continuing the war and desired a cease-fire.

I asked that anything else was discussed by Iraq at the 1991 cease-fire talks. Hussein stated that he does not remember any additional Iraqi request other than the withdrawal of foreign forces from their territory. And Hussein's opinion the fighting would have continued without this withdrawal. Hussein denied knowledge that Iraq asked for, and received permission to continue flying helicopters. He further denied knowledge of the purpose of such an Iraqi request.

Chapter 10

Cease Fire 1991

After the cease-fire of 1991, Hussein stated the goal of the Iraqi leadership was the rebuilding of the infrastructure of Iraq destroyed during the war. This included reconstituting agricultural and economic programs. Hussein stated that Iraqi rebuilt "almost everything" and started new programs in the areas of agriculture, education, and health. However, Iraq's efforts were hampered by the embargo particularly affecting the health and education sectors.

When pointed out to Hussein that several changes were made in the eye Iraqi government around this time including appointment of individuals to new positions, Hussein stated, "This is natural." In his opinion, such changes are "regular" occurrences not only in Iraq but also in countries such as the United States. One such appointee, Abid Hamid Mahmoud, became Hussein's personal secretary at this time replacing the previous secretary who had been appointed as Iraqi Minister of Education. Hussein referred to Mahmoud as a "senior companion of mine" who had served as a member of the president's protective detail in Himaya and Murafiqeen. Another individual, Tariq Aziz, was named as Iraqi Deputy Prime Minister. Hussein described Aziz as one of the early revolutionary command Council (RCC) members. In Hussein's opinion, Aziz "did not gain anything" with this appointment. Hussein stated that he told the Iraqi leadership if he (Hussein) was to also have the title as Iraqi Prime Minister, he would need assistance from others. Thus, Aziz and Taha Yasin Ramadan were named as deputy Prime Minister's.

Hussein explained that the duties of a personal secretary include arranging the schedule of the person for whom the person is working. A secretary must be precise and executing his duties. Hussein selected Mahmoud as his personal secretary because he was "suitable for the position." He added that this was his own choice and not a matter of historical significance. Hussein reiterated that Mahmoud had served in the Himaya and Murafiqeen, and that both organizations were composed of Hussein's relatives. At the beginning of the revolution, only one of his relatives served in an Iraqi government political position. At that time, Hussein's relatives had limited education and primarily served in the Iraqi Army and other military services.

Hussein pointed out that members of his protective detail did not necessarily dictate the details of his movements. He claimed that at times, he taught them ways to improve their performance and be more successful. He recalled joking with them that he could perform their job better. He felt it was very important that detail members not to be "rough" when Hussein "mingled" with other people. In his opinion, the detail would have failed in its mission if it "isolated" him from the masses. It was also important that the detail be able to alter their duties and behavior to accommodate Hussein's nature. As further evidence of his teaching abilities, Hussein stated that if requested, he could provide advice regarding the writers interviewing details. When asked to expound on this statement, Hussein said, "A doctor does not chase people asking them what is wrong. They come to him."

Hussein stated that the most important thing is to look at one's position, whether executing our planning, to determine how to perform duties. A person executing orders must be precise and quick. One whose surveys must allow those under him to exercise initiative. The "margin for initiative" differs between civilian and military situations. Hussein stated, "The eyes in the field are different than those at headquarters." Often, the "field eyes" are more accurate and understanding the particular situation then headquarters components.

When asked what character traits he seeks in subordinates, Hussein stated, "a human being is not like merchandise." One may think an individual is suitable for a position only to later discover that he does not possess the desirable traits. According to Hussein, a particular situation may require a selection of a particular individual even though, under other circumstances, this individual may not be considered the best choice. This is particularly true in the context of selecting the right person for military operations.

Hussein explained that the selection or dismissal of individuals for particular military government positions often involves consideration of the perception of one's family or tribe. Another factor to consider is the strength of the Iraqi psych and sense of "individuality." Although a particular situation may necessitate the removal of an Iraqi from his position, a leader must consider how this individual's removal may be perceived. For example, relatives of the individual removed from office may question the individual's character. Some will ask "again and again" why the individual was dismissed. Others may ask, "Was he a coward?" These questions may even be asked when an individual decides to retire under normal circumstances. The families of such individuals may feel "tainted." Under some circumstances, such actions may cause families to hate the government. Hussein explained that in having to consider these feelings and attitudes, military and governmental leaders were often limited to making personal changes, even if they were deemed necessary.

I asked about the commonly reported uprisings which occurred in southern Iraq after the war in 1991, Hussein claimed that he had not heard of any such uprisings. When it was pointed out that many interviews and reports had documented the uprisings, Hussein asked, "Have we not discuss this matter?" He stated, however, that within a day of the cease-fire of 1991, "some elements" had initiated sabotage operations in the southern Iraqi cities of Basra, Nasiriyah, and Amarah. Later, this activity spread to the northern cities of Suleimaniyah, Erbil, and Kirkuk. Hussein stated that the groups conducting these operations were "punished by Iran," and that Iraq captured 68 Iranian intelligence officers who were later exchange for Iraqi prisoners.

At the time of the uprising, most bridges in Iraq had already been destroyed. Electricity did not exist. Water service was sporadic, and food supplies were minimal. In the aftermath of the war, these factors contributed to general unrest in the country. Hussein stated that "elements" participating in the uprising were a mixture of thieves, rebels, and "those from Iran." The latter group included individuals from Iranian government services, Iraqis of Iranian origin, and Iraqis who had "escaped" to Iran. Their nationalities were difficult to determine with any degree of certainty because many had intentionally destroyed their citizenship documents.

Hussein stated that after deciding to reassert government control of the country, the Iraqi leadership considered the southern area of Iraq to be a high priority. It was in this area where Iraqi forces encountered and fought primarily Iranians. After order was restored in southern Iraq, government forces focused on the northern region where Iraq he forces meant little or no resistance. The fighting in the North and the South lasted approximately 2 months. Hussein stated "God made us victorious." Thereafter, according to Hussein, I ran continued to insert groups of 10 to 15 people into Iraq to conduct operations against the government. However, these individuals were, for the most part, thwarted by members of the local population. Ultimately, following an agreement between Iran and Iraq, these hostile operations ceased.

Hussein characterize the uprisings in 1991 as insurgent activity conducted by "outlaws and thieves." He did not consider the insurgents to be revolutionaries. When asked what factors allow these disturbances, Hussein answered that it was port from Iran, weakness of the Iraqi government after the war, and possibly assistance from coalition forces. He noted that all government institutions including the police and the military had been weakened as a result of the war. Gradually however, the Iraqi military grew in strength, and they were eventually able to overcome these rebels. According to the saying, the Iraqi militaries "blade got longer and longer." He acknowledged, however, that though weakened state of the Iraqi military had been the main factor which provided the opportunity for the lawlessness in the first place.

Hussein believed the goal of the insurgent activity was to control Iraq. In his opinion, this tactic was utilized in 1991 after I ran had been unable to accomplish this goal through its previous war with Iraq. Iran had wanted to control all or what at least a part of Iraq, particularly the southern portion. It was Hussein's belief that your Randall also wanted to extend its power to eastern Saudi Arabia and into the entire Gulf region.

The RCC gave the Iraqi provincial governors control of the military during the uprising in order to protect the people and the state and to reestablish security and a "normal life." The people and the nation were threatened by widespread killings, theft, arson, and general destruction, all of which had to be brought under control. Hussein denied knowledge of the methods used by the government and the military to reassert control. Hussein stated, "They were given the authority, and they carried it out." At the time, he did not ask for details of the operation, but he did request and receive status reports regarding the progression of operations.

Regarding the limitations placed on the Iraqi military by the leadership during this time period, Hussein asked, "what do you mean by limits?" Hussein denied that the Geneva Convention applied to this situation, claiming it only applied to wars. Hussein claimed that with respect to internal conflicts the Geneva Convention applied only to situations when an occupying power is another country. He claimed that the Geneva Convention was applicable to attempt crews and internal unrest involving crimes such as burning and looting.

Pointed out to Hussein that international law does not permit the targeting of civilians even when the location of a military objective is populated by civilians in that certain laws of humanity always apply. When asked again what restrictions were placed on the Iraqi military during the 1991 uprisings? Hussein replied that an Iraqi, whether civilian or military, knows what is acceptable as human behavior, and there is no need for someone to have to tell them how to behave.

Hussein stated, "I am responsible for what I decide." He added that he is not responsible for how an Iraqi acts. Hussein claimed that if in Iraq he wanted to use him (Hussein) as the justification for his actions, he would accept that ascertain shouldn't so long as it does not harm Hussein's reputation. And Hussein's opinion a leader is responsible for the actions of a subordinate if he becomes aware of that subordinates transgressions and confronts him about the wrongfulness of his actions. He stated that each individual is judged based on his own law and constitution.

Hussein stated that he was made aware of the details regarding the situation in southern Iraq in the same fashion as any leader of a country. Whenever faced with the situation, the Iraqi leadership assembled and consulted "quickly" about the best manner in which to confront an issue.

Hussein stated that, initially, those who carry out acts during the uprising in southern Iraq were among "those who had crossed the border from Iran." Others from Iraq committed similar acts, while some were not involved at all in the incidents. According to Hussein, if the Iraqi government response to these actions had been slow and weak, some individuals might have shown sympathy and assisted the participants in the uprising. Without such a response, they might have acted out of fear thinking that those who caused disturbances would ultimately rise to power in the Iraqi government. In addition, other individuals Hussein described as "greedy thieves and robbers" might have participated in the uprisings.

Hussein asserted that it was the duty of the Iraqi government to confront the individuals participated in the uprisings. Hussein stated that although the "arms of the authorities had been severed" by the 1991 war, the Iraqi government "pick them up and struck the enemy." He added that those who would not be deterred by words would be deterred by weapons. The Iraqi leadership ordered the army to a symbol as many forces as possible in order to confront "treachery" and the disturbances. Hussein acknowledged that incidents of looting by certain individuals "got mixed in" with the actions of those participating in the uprisings.

When asked about certain individuals in charge of areas in southern Iraq during this time. And their assigned roles, Hussein replied, "I said our decisions was to confront and defeat the enemy." The participants in the uprisings were to be "put in their place," if not by word then by weapons. Hussein stated that a lengthy discussion of this matter was not required. The individual who had crossed the border from Iran were members of the Dawa Party. They were assisted by additional Iranian forces. Together, these individuals killed, burn, looted, and commit other crimes. According to Hussein, one does not need to ask what actions should be taken when faced with such a situation. Procedure, however, dictated that the Iraqi leadership meet to discuss the matter. All members of the leadership held the same opinion regarding the Iraqi government response required to deal with this situation. When asked how information was communicated to him regarding events occurring in southern Iraq and regarding subsequent responses by Iraqi government forces, Hussein asked, "With Iraq being so small, is it possible we wouldn't know what was going on?" He added that the entire population of southern Iraq began migrating to Baghdad during this time period. Information from one of the Iraqi commanders in the South, Ali Hassan Al-Majid, was "cut off" and was not reaching the Iraqi leadership. Soon after, it became clear to the leadership that Al-Majid was "resisting" in Basra.

When asked whether reports were true about Al-Majid was actually trapped in Basra at this time, Hussein responded "in the past, Iraqi did not respect law and authority." When called to military service, Iraqis generally failed to respond. When called for "questioning," Iraqis also generally failed to respond. According to Hussein, national rule was a relatively new concept during this time period. Even though most Iraqis were Arab, they were not accustomed to being ruled by an Arab, in this case King Faisal at that time. He was "installed" into power by the British. The disregard for law was particularly prevalent in rule areas at that time.

Hussein then provided details of a story about an individual named Madhi Ubaid and his son who was wanted by the government. As a result of a police operation, Ubaid was captured and interrogated regarding the whereabouts of his son. Ubaid responded, "I have no son." The police asked, "Are you Madhi?" Ubaid replied, "no, I Fadhi." The police slapped him and told Ubaid "you are Madhi." Thereafter, Ubaid stated, "If the government says I'm Madhi, I'm Mahdi." Hussein ended the discussion of Al – Majid's situation Basra stating, "You heard what you heard. I heard what I heard."

Hussein stated that the threat to the Iraqi government 1991 existed in both northern and southern Iraq. And uprising was even attempt to Baghdad. Hussein Opined that those "sitting on the fence" joined in the uprising upon seeing police stations and government officials attacked with no resistance by the authorities. As the Iraqi government reasserted control, the "enemy" wit to a new error or reinforced in an old one. According to Hussein, the Iraqi military strength grew over time and "the circle started tightening around the enemy."

Hussein noted that the previous period of lawlessness he discussed, during Mahdi's time, was in the 1920s. He added that the attitude of the Iraqis changed completely during the last 35 years under the Ba'ath Party. In Hussein's opinion, with a political Party present throughout Iraq, then Iraqi people believed in the government agenda, had faith in their leadership, and would be more disciplined than ever before. This led to an improvement in the situation in Iraq, particularly in the economy. According to Hussein, no "poor person" existed in Iraq in the 1980s. Widows, orphans, and other elderly were "taking care of and secure." Commercial products were relatively inexpensive. This eye Iraqi lifestyle diminished however, around the midpoint of the Iran Iraq war and after the 1991 Gulf War. Hussein stated, "An embargo is an embargo." After the downturn in the economy, employees, and Iraqi citizens in general were less disciplined. However their allegations did not change.

Hussein acknowledge that Iraq was on its way to becoming economically strong in the mid-early 1980s. He added that all the positive things Iraq had been created by the leadership. Hussein further acknowledge that the economic situation deteriorated dramatically in the 1980s. Hussein agreed that the decline in the Iraqi economy at that time and the subsequent 1991 Gulf War which led to embargoes and United Nations (UN) inspections lesson the economy strength of the country. He acknowledged that this decline was felt by the Iraqi people especially among those in rule areas and among lower income individuals such as those living in southern Iraq. Hussein added that the central and northern areas of Iraq were also affected.

Hussein acknowledge that, as a general rule, the pressures of poverty can greatly strained a society possibly leading to revolution. However, he provided several examples of situations involving revolutions in Iraq and other countries in the Arab world which did not stem from economic conditions. Hussein stated that acts of insurgency without a political goal, such as those which occurred in 1991, are not revolutions.

I noted to Hussein that various neutral and nongovernmental and humanitarian organizations conducted investigations of the actions of the Iraqi military during the uprising in the 1991 war. One such investigation conducted by human rights watch (HRW), a neutral nonprofit organization not associated with any government, provided details about Iraqi military actions. I read Hussein a summary of an HRW interview of a resident in Basra who witness one such event in 1991. According to the witness, he saw a column of the Iraqi tanks approaching Basra. The lead tank had three children tied to its front being forced to act as a human shields. When questioned regarding his knowledge of such actions of the Iraqi military in 1991, Hussein replied that even though he believes this information does not deserve a reply, he would answer for my benefit. Hussein stated, "It's a lie." He added that, in Iraq, each child has a father, a mother, and a family. Iraq "does not have orphans walking the streets." Regarding these three children, Hussein asked, "Where were their parents?" He questioned why I would accept that a tank commander what act so irresponsibly. Hussein further asked why the tactic of using children as human shields would have been considered effective against those who were already killing, looting, and burning. He added that a story about using children in this manner may have been fabricated by Westerners. Hussein reiterated that the story did not deserve an answer from him and "That Lie Is Clear."

Chapter 11

Southern Iraq Uprisings

A television documentary was shown to Hussein with regards to the situation in southern Iraq in 1991 in the aftermath of the first Gulf War. Hussein provided comments before viewing this documentation. He stated that each person presents information from a certain background, based upon his beliefs and life experiences. Despite having his own opinion, a person is affected by the thoughts of others. Any person presenting information on Iraq or any other country speaks from three points of view. The first is a "divine scale" according to his own beliefs the second is a skill based upon his life experiences in his own country. The third and final viewpoint is based on what is known by the person regarding information from the United Nations (UN) and the international law. Hussein then asked me. "What is your scale as you show the film?" Hussein offered that this information would enable him to comment and answer questions in that best manner.

I told Hussein that one must listen to all the facts and find out the truth. Hussein asked, "How will you know the truth?" Quote he added that I would be using Western media, possibly biased, to determine the truth. Hussein stated, "Your army occupies my country. You are free. I am a prisoner." He added that one who searches for the truth must directly contact the people who are involved in the matter of concern. In the instance of southern Iraq in 1991 after the war, Hussein stated one would have to speak to "those who were violated, such as women, "by those who were sent to Iran.

Those same individuals sent by Iran committee other acts in southern Iraq include looting, burning and killing Hussein stated that one should contact others who share his (Hussein's) opinion.

Hussein opined that documentation such as this, prepared in the West and first broadcast in America, is not a neutral film production by neutral individuals. He added that the film is likely based upon the teachings of Christ, the laws of the United States, international law, and life in the United States. Hussein emphasize that he did not want to put me in a difficult position. He added that I must "learn the truth as it is" not as Hussein tells it, nor as the film producers tell.

I then started the approximate one hour documentary. Hussein stated that the scenes showing Shias in southern Iraq "could be seen anywhere, even now." He stated that Shais shown in Karbala in the mosque were not confined and surrounded, as depicted. In reference to the reporters words regarding scenes showing Iraqi tanks approaching the mosque, Hussein asked, "where are the tanks?" He added that a statement in the documentary indicating that President Bush "encourage" the Shias to rise up against the Iraqi government is "a confession of the crime."

Hussein asked me the various questions including the date of the documentary. The name of the commentator, and the name of the nongovernmental organization from whom the reporter work.

Hussein regarded the scene showing Shias who had fled southern Iraq and traveled to Kurdish territory in northern Iraq, Hussein stated these individuals "do not appear to base scared, they appear to be happy." He added that these individuals looked Kurdish, not Shia.

After viewing approximately 23 minutes of the documentary, Hussein stated that his exercise time and prayer time had arrived. When I told him that his exercise. Could be postponed until later in the day, he replied "I think it is enough so far." Hussein added that the documentary could be viewed another day and asked, "Why rush?"

Hussein then provided several comments without further prompting or questioning. He noted that the documentary stated the Shia rose up against the Iraqi government with the encouragement of President Bush. Hussein stated that though "traders rose up at the order of a foreign country" and declared war on their own country.

Hussein stated that the interview of Shia Ayatollah Khoei demonstrates a contradiction in the truth. According to the commentator, Khoei believes in the peaceful aspect of his religion. Hussein stated Khoei's replied to the commentators question indicates he does not agree with mixing of politics and terror/violence. According to Hussein, this is in direct contradiction to the actions of the Shia.

Regarding the film's depiction of Shia conduct, Hussein reiterated space "we cannot see this anywhere." Hussein stated that if an insurgent does not surrender his weapon, he will be confronted with force. He added that the Shiite use the Iman Hussein shrine in Karbala as a headquarters for their resistance. Hussein stated that the blood shown on the inside walls of the shrine was from Iraqi "comrades" executed in the building and not from Shias killed during the Iraqi government assault.

Hussein stated that the individual shown in the film whose time has reportedly cut out may have simply been a mute. The documentary provided no information about why or who cut his tongue, other than Iraqi military intelligence.

Hussein opined that they Kurdish individuals shown walking and departing their villages may have been "migrating." He added that they may have been moving to avoid a combat zone.

Hussein asked whether the commentator question that Shias regarding the things they lost when the "criminals came in occupied their city." He stated that he felt sorry for someone who watches this documentary and does not know the truth. Hussein asked rhetorically "how would someone know the Shia would act this way about something what happened 1300 years ago?"

Made in 1993, the film is titled "Saddam Hussein's latest war" and is narrated by British Commentator Michael would.

As Hussein viewed the documentary he questioned the source of the figure 300,000 provided by the speaker in the documentary as an estimated number of Shias killed in southern Iraq by Iraqi government. I noted to him that this figure had been discussed during the portion of the documentary viewed in the previous session and its source was the Iraqi government. According to the film, the Iraqi government informed the Kurds at this number of Shia's had been killed. I added that this message from the Iraqi government is believed to have been intended as a warning to the Kurds not to defy the government.

The film also depicted scenes of the Iraqi government actions against the marsh Arabs in southern Iraq including the poisoning of water resulting in the killing of fish, the destruction of villages, and the draining of the marshes. Hussein commented that some of the scenes shown did not appear to have been filmed at the site of the marshes. As the documentary continued, one scene showed a marsh Arab female commenting the treatment of her people by the Iraqi government. She stated that they had nothing left and had to leave their homes with only a few possessions. Hussein laughed and asked, "What did she have before? Reeds?"

The documentary then showed additional scenes and provided commentary about the Iraqi government's treatment of the Shias in southern Iraq, the Kurds in the northern Iraq, and the marsh Arabs. The film discussed the possibility of placing Hussein on trial for these atrocities. Hussein stated, "now that they have apprehended me, let them put me on trial."

The film then ended after a total of approximately 55 bins and 50 seconds. Upon asking me, Hussein was informed this documentary was made in 1993. I regarded the assignment of certain senior Iraqi leaders to positions in southern Iraq in 1991 who were to bear the responsibility of dealing with the Shia uprising, Hussein stated, "We assigned responsibility to whoever was going to handle the situation." Hussein denied that he previously stated that he did not want to know the details of how the uprising would be stopped and what he only wanted to know was the results. Hussein asked, "who says I did not want to know how?) Upon being informed by me that Hussein made this previous ascertain he stated that any person's main goal would have been to stop the disturbances and two and the "treason."

I noted that this documentary shows the cost, human and otherwise, of stopping the treason. Hussein stated that nothing was shown on this film. According to Hussein, it shows individuals who were apprehended by the Iraqi government and some government official who "behaved in a wrong manner when they struck them." He acknowledged that the documentary shows scenes of other topics.

The conversation turned to the discussion about the definition of treason versus a revolution. I reminded Hussein that he had observed a portion of the film in the previous session claiming that President Bush encouraged the Shia to revolt against the Iraqi government 1991. I then further reminded him that Hussein previously stated that the Shia, after Bush's encouragement, turned against their own country and that Hussein previously stated he considered the Shia to be traitors. I also noted that some would describe the Ba'ath Party in the same fashion regarding various coup attempts and successful coups in 1959, 1963, and 1968. I then further noted to Hussein that some described a failed uprising as treason, while a successful one is viewed as a revolution. Hussein stated, "I do not have a comment." He added that it was "beneath him" to comment about this documentary. Hussein characterize the film as not being objective and he opined that it was made as further justification for "what was being done against Iraq" including the partitioning of the country.

Hussein stated that an accused individual should be allowed to defend himself. He asked whether Iraqi was afforded the opportunity to defend itself regarding the information in the film. Hussein questioned the appropriateness of interviewing the Pres. of Iraq about such a propaganda film. He added, "We should stop this program." Hussein asserted that he had answered all of my questions. He affirmed that he would not comment on such propaganda films again.

Hussein acknowledge that Mohammed Hamza AL-Zubaidi and Kamal Mustapha Abdallah were sent to Nasiriya in 1991 to confront the Shia uprising in that area. Similarly, Hussein Kamil was sent to Karbala, Ali Hasan Al-Majid was sent to Basra, and Izzat Ibrahim Al-Duri was sent to Al-Hilla.

Hussein described Al-Zubaid as a "Comrade in our Party." Who had reached the leadership position of Prime Minister. Hussein stated that he considers every Iraqi to be a good person until that person demonstrates otherwise to him. He characterized-Zubaidi "good." Hussein acknowledge that Al-Zubaid was one of the few Shia in the Iraqi senior leadership. When asked whether Al-Zubaid was respected by his colleagues, Hussein said, "That is another thing, something different." Hussein refused to explain this comment any further. He added, as previously stated, that he will only say good things about his comrades. Based upon Hussein's answer, I stated that one might presume that Al-Zubaid was not in good standing with his colleagues. Hussein replied that I could presume as I wished, positively or negatively, about Al-Zubaid. He added, "I gave my answer."

Hussein acknowledge that Abdallah was a distant cousin and a member of the Ba'ath Party. He stated that Abdallah served as an officer in the Iraqi army but was not "in the government." Abdallah assume the same duties as any other military officer in the army. Hussein stated that he does not remember the location of Abdallah's assignments. When asked whether Abdallah held the position of Sec. General of the Republican guard (RG) the special Republican guard (SR G), Hussein replied, "I thought the questions related to what happened in the South." I noted that Hussein's perspective on members of the Iraqi leadership is important. Hussein reiterated that he has faith and trust in anyone, whether in the Party, the government, or the military, until that person "behaves badly." He added that if he does not describe someone as "bad" that means that person is good. Hussein further characterized a "bad" person as someone who behaves in a manner contrary to the trust existing between him and the other person.

Hussein stated that during the war with Iran, the RG assume duties on the front lines leaving Baghdad in the presidential Palace unguarded. Thus, that is RG was formed, first of companies, then with regiments. At that time, many young officer served in the SRG including Abdallah. He would later become commander of the SR G. However, the commanders of the SR G and RG were not necessarily Hussein's relatives. Abdallah was one of the many individuals in the eye Iraqi leadership. Hussein stated that Abdallah preformed his duties as would any other officer.

I questioned about the instruction given by the Iraqi leadership to Al-Zubaidi and Abdallah regarding the response necessary for the Shia uprising in southern Iraq, Hussein stated, "I explained during the last meeting." Hussein added that during the last session he also explained how information regarding the situation in southern Iraq in 1991 was communicated back to the Iraqi leadership. I noted to Hussein that Al-Zubaidi and Abdallah are in the custody of coalition forces. Hussein stated, "What do I want from them?" He asked rhetorically, "do you think I would answer based upon who is in custody?" He added, "I am afraid of no one. I am only afraid of God." Hussein stated his answers are not based upon who is in custody but upon what he believes to be the truth. His answers are not dependent upon who is alive or dead. Hussein stated that he is not the type of person who would blame someone because that person is dead, such as blaming the late Hussein Kamil. He added, "I will only talk about myself." Hussein recommended that I talk directly to Al-Zubaidi and Abdallah as they "know themselves better."

94

Hussein reiterated a statement made during a previous interview saying "any person answering you who, if it lessened their burden, and it does not harm my reputation, I will accept."

I ended the questioning that day telling Hussein that I did not wish to further delay his prayer and mealtime. Hussein stated, "Any government, if it is to lessen it sends in the eyes of God, then it should do so." He added, "The sins of the US government are not few." Hussein ended the session by saying that it was good that I did not prevent him from praying, as this would be one less sin on my shoulders.

Chapter 11

Shia Uprisings in Southern Iraq

Prior to the start of the interview, Hussein advised that today's discussion would be a continuation of previous meetings regarding the Shia uprisings in southern in 1991.

Hussein stated that it is natural for the leader of a political Party, such as the Ba'ath, to attempt to know as many members of the Party as possible. For Hussein, however, it was difficult to become acquainted with Ba'ath Party members outside of the senior leadership. Nevertheless Hussein attempted to know as many members of the Party as possible, just as he tried to meet many individuals of the general population of Iraq.

I asked about the communication system between the various levels of the Party from the local to the national level and how much information the Iraqi senior leadership actually saw. Hussein stated that the Iraqi senior leaders received information regarding their Party much in the same manner as Democrats and Republicans in America. When a directive was issued by the leadership, instructions were sent to all Party members. When a Party member desired a certain action, a request was submitted through the appropriate channels to the Iraqi leadership. Hussein was questioned about his feelings regarding the importance of Party members informing him of the local situation. He stated, "There is a difference between desire and what is possible."

I stated that a number of documents describing the 1991 uprisings and Ba'ath Party activities during this period were recovered after the invasion of coalition forces in 2003. The translator read to Hussein portions of copies of two documents written in Arabic. One document, dated April 11, 1991, described as report number 7/1/383, signed by Hussein Hamza .Abbas, Secretary General of the Saddam Section Command, was sent to the Secretary General of the Wasit Section Command. According to the document, Abbas wrote the letter to explain and clarify his conduct during the "disturbances" of March, 1991. The second document, dated April, 1991, bearing no report number, signed by Anwar Saeed Omar, Secretary General of the Wasit Section Command, was directed to an unstated, but presumably, higher command element. This document explains certain actions taken during "disturbances" in the cities of Basra and Wasit in March, 1991 including the arrest of approximately 700 military and civilian suspects in Basra. In the letter, Omar states that interrogation committees were formed and that he was put in charge of the Second Corps Committee. Omar writes that he personally executed two individuals on the same day h began interrogations. He further states that an additional forty-two individuals were executed after four more days of interrogation.

When questioned about .the seeming contradiction in the actions described in these documents and Iraq's justice system, Hussein asked, "Where is the contradiction?" He added that committees were formed, questioning occurred, and judgment was passed. Hussein asked, "What was the alternative?" I noted to Hussein that the documents appear to describe a situation where individuals were not investigated by a neutral entity. The necessity of a neutral investigative body was previously discussed by Hussein with respect to the situation in Kuwait and crimes reportedly committed by the Iraqi military during occupation of the country in 1991. I

97

further noted that the individuals appeared not to have the chance to defend themselves, as also previously mentioned by Hussein as being important. Hussein stated, "I did not say anything about Kuwaitis." He commented that Kuwait and this issue are "two different things." These documents discuss acts of "treachery and sabotage." Hussein stated that it appears that the individuals did have a chance to defend themselves. I noted that it appears the two individuals mentioned were not given the opportunity to defend themselves and were executed on the spot. Hussein responded, "Possibly. Possibly not."   He added that this is a report which may not have included all the details. Hussein stated the author may have been simply bragging to show his loyalty and ability to accomplish a task.   He questioned the validity of this report. If true, Hussein stated that when the time comes and America decides to place the individuals captured for these crimes on .trial and Iraqis have resumed leadership of the country, Iraqis will investigate this matter.

Hussein questioned what right I had to ask about internal Iraqi events of 1991. He asked, "Is it because you are an employee of the American government?" I noted that he is attempting to separate fact from fiction and to record history as it occurred.

Hussein stated that it was difficult to comment on the referenced documents without the full details. He questioned my assertion that the two individuals discussed in the one document were not allowed to defend themselves. Hussein further questioned whether the individuals were even executed.

As stated in a previous interview, Hussein acknowledged that he had lived with the Marsh Arabs for a short period of time. While Hussein was in Egypt in the early 1960s, he hoped that it was "God's will" that he would return to Iraq.

Upon returning, Hussein attempted to. Expand his own knowledge of Iraq through actual experience in areas of the country where he had never spent significant time including the mountains and the marshes. Hussein described life in the marshes of southern Iraq as "enchanted for any human being. "The summers, however, were not pleasant due to the oppressive heat and humidity as well as the presence of insects.

Regarding the drainage of the marshes conducted by the Iraqi government, Hussein stated that one was faced with the choice of preserving nature at the expense of humans or sacrificing a bit of nature for the sake of humans. Hussein noted that the water in the inhabited parts of the marshes was not always clean due to human and animal pollution. The inhabitants of the marshes drank this water and bathed in it. As a result, illness was prevalent including widespread bilharzias is, an intestinal disease. Life expectancy was relatively low. Hussein stated the Iraqi government could not simply "sit back and watch this misery. "He added that the government decided to "bring them inside life" or to modernize the Marsh Arabs way of life. Hussein reiterated the difficult choice of the Iraqi government to preserve the simple, primitive life of the Marsh inhabitants or to bring them within the framework of modern life where a human is not "disgraced or insulted."

Hussein stated that all of Iraq is beautiful and again described the marshes as "enchanted." He added, "I slept there for days in 1981 and 1982." During that time period, Hussein stated he would travel to the front lines of the Iran- Iraq War in the morning, then return to the marshes in the evening upon completion of his duties. Hussein described this period as "the best of days." He claimed that he spent parts of each year from 1978-84 visiting the marshes.

Hussein described his visit in 1980 of a village called Baida located in the middle of the marshes. According to information, residents of Baida attacked a police station.

Hussein stated this was not a matter •to handle in a simple fashion. He traveled to Baida in a Party of three boats, one carrying Hussein and others, one carrying his protective detail, and one carrying "news people. "This event was filmed and shown on television. •According to Hussein, the residents of Baida were "happy to see us." They slaughtered animals and prepared a meal thinking Hussein and his entourage would stay for dinner.

However, the group only remained for a three hours then departed. Hussein never asked the residents of Baida whether they attacked a police station. At the time, Hussein was questioned by a member of his protective detail regarding the necessity for an investigation of the participation of the residents of Baida in the attack. In response, he stated, "Good people understood me. The evil ones also got the message. "Hussein added that if a similar act had subsequently occurred, they would be "dealt with properly."

Hussein stated that the Iraqi government had good relations with the Marsh Arabs. However, upon entry of a foreigner into the situation, "it becomes bad. "Husscin asserted that some of the Marsh Arabs were corrupted by Iran. In particular, the area of the Hweiza marshes became a smuggling route beginning during the time of the Shah of Iran. Hussein suggested that the family seen in the video previously shown by me was from Hweiza.

Hussein stated the Iraqi government chose to drain the marshes for the sake of the inhabitants and for strategic reasons for Iraq.He reiterated the. Iraqi government wanted to modernize the way of life for the Marsh Arabs so that they would "not live like animals. "Hussein believed it was unfit for an Iraqi to live in these conditions. The drainage of the marshes was also conducted for a strategic purpose. Only one road existed connecting Basra to Amarah to Baghdad. At points, this road was completely surrounded by the marshes. When the Iranians entered Iraq in 1984, their main goal was to cut off this road and to isolate Basra. Accordingly, the Iraqi government decided to drain the marshes and build a detour providing a secondary route.

The Iraqi government studied the idea of building homes in the marshes for the inhabitants. However, research showed that this project would be too expensive and complicated particularly in the areas of sewage and electricity. As a result, the idea was abandoned and the government decided to build housing complexes on dry land or the displaced Marsh Arabs. The residents were also offered monetary allowances to build their own homes. Hussein stated that the government provided water, electricity, health care services, and schools for the inhabitants. Previously, teachers and medical professionals would refuse to enter the marshes unless paid three to four times their normal salaries.

Hussein described the marshes as "nice to visit for two, three, or four days." In the summer, however, mosquitos would "eat you" and life was very harsh. Hussein acknowledged that humans have a need for primitive life, but only for a few days at a time. He added that the older man previously seen in the film commenting about the Marsh Arabs "came as a visitor, but did not live there" nor did his wife and children.

Hussein suggested that I should talk to personnel of the Iraqi Ministry of Irrigation in order to understand how the drainage was implemented. He added that the task was accomplished within three to four months. Regarding the individual or individuals who designed and supervised the marsh drainage, Hussein stated the Iraqi government utilized the entities with the most expertise and the necessary equipment.

The project included the involvement of the Ministry of Housing, the Ministry of Irrigation and possibly the city of Baghdad.

The entire nation" and many of its experts participated in the drainage of the marshes. When noted to Hussein that Muhammad Hamza Al-Zubaidi claimed to be the architect" of the marsh drainage who first proposed such a plan to the Iraqi Revolutionary Command Council (RCC) in 1991, Hussein responded, "Maybe." Hussein stated, however, that he received the first plan and proposal from Hussein Kamil. He is unaware whether Kamil consulted with Al-Zubaidi regarding the project.

Similarly, Hussein denied knowledge whether Al-Zubaidi discussed the marsh drainage with other Iraqi leaders. He added, "If he (Al-Zubaidi) said this, he is being truthful." I told Hussein that others had also claimed to be the originators of the idea of the drainage of the marshes. Hussein replied that it is understandable that any Iraqi might attempt to take credit for such an important task that improved the lives of the Marsh Arabs while simultaneously cutting off the path of a foe such as Iran.

When questioned about reports of the presence of Iraqi army deserters and saboteurs in the marshes in 1991 and steps taken by the Iraqi government to deal with these individuals, Hussein acknowledged the existence of deserters. As typical for any protracted conflict, •some individuals decide to abandon their duties. This has occurred in the past and continues to occur today during war. For a deserter, the Iraqi law is applied or the individual is pardoned by the appropriate authority. Hussein stated that the presence of deserters in the marshes of southern Iraq was not a contributing factor which led to the drainage.

Hussein stated that saboteurs began using the marshes after 1991. The response of the Iraqi government was "the same as that of any government against those who violate the law. "Hussein could provide no example of a government response to saboteur activity. He denied that a military plan existed for confronting saboteurs and deserters. He stated that deserters were typically pursued by the police, local citizens, and family members. In cases of mutiny such as that which existed in 1991, Hussein stated the army would intervene. Hussein acknowledged that there were probably times when the Iraqi military had to deal with saboteurs.

When questioned whether the historical value of the marshes was considered prior to the drainage, Hussein asked whether similar consideration was given to the area where the High Dam was built in Egypt. He added that ruins located in the area of the dam were moved prior to construction. Hussein opined that some discussion most likely took place regarding issues concerning the movement of the stones versus saving the people from starvation. He stated that the .matter of the drainage of the marshes "was studied" and "there is no historical value of the marshes."

Regarding any consideration given by the Iraqi government to the environmental impact of the drainage of the marshes, Hussein replied that he could debate this matter with experts for "the next twenty days." He noted that Americans did not allow the Indians to live as they had existed prior to colonization. He asked what laws are in place which prohibit American and European companies from destroying the jungles of the Amazon, which he described as the "lungs of the earth." Hussein asked, "Do we preserve species of birds and other animals or do we worry about the existence of Iraqis?" He further asked whether the water of the marshes should have been wasted for the sake of preserving the marshes or used for agriculture. Hussein stated, "What we did was correct. "He added, if not, Americans should reopen the water now. I noted that a recent news article reported local Iraqi citizens did, in fact, recently collect money, rented a bulldozer, and opened a part of the canal in order to allow water to flow back into the marshes.

Chapter 12

Casual Conversations

Hussein inquired on current events in Iraq. Hussein was advised of the accomplishments in Iraq, to include the signing of the new constitution, .and the preparations for the turnover of sovereignty to the Iraqis. Hussein questioned the effectiveness of the Governing Council (GC), in his view the GC could agree among themselves to make decisions Hussein was advised of the eventual elections in Iraq, in which the Iraqi people will have the opportunity to democratically elect a new leader. Hussein stated that the Iraqi people would not accept an elected leader during occupation and has experienced this in the past when King Faisal was brought to power under British power.

It was described to Hussein the recent poll of Iraqis in which the Iraqi people want control over their government, but want United States forces to remain in Iraq.

While talking about the air conditioning in Hussein's cell, which was being repaired at that time, Hussein advised that he is used to living simply and personally does not like an extravagant lifestyle. Hussein was then questioned about the number of palaces and their extravagant nature. Hussein stated that the palaces belong to the nation and not to one person. Before 1968, the Iraqi homes were basically very primitive and made out of mud. As in western countries, historically architects developed their skill and designs by building castles. The palaces gave Iraqi architects the opportunity to

105

develop their skills which could then be seen in the improvement of the design of the typical Iraqi home.

Additionally, there was a threat from the United States and Israel, especially during the last ten years. For the government to function, the leadership had to meet and discuss issues prior to rendering decisions. If there were only two palaces or locations that the leadership could meet, it would have been very easy for the elimination of the Iraqi leadership. However, with twenty palaces, it was much more difficult to track or identify the location of the Iraqi leadership. Since these palaces belonged to the nation, Hussein did not live in them and preferred to live in a simple home. Hussein would eat what was prepared for his protection detail and did not have a lot of demands. Hussein believed the United States had a misconception that he had an extravagant lifestyle, which lead to his ability to evade capture. Hussein believes •his capture was solely caused by betrayal.

Hussein's work schedule was long, but he would set time aside for fictional reading, something he enjoyed very much. His days would include meetings with the other senior Ba'ath Party members. Hussein claimed he regularly met with the Iraqi people as he found them to be the best source of accurate information. Hussein would meet with citizens daily, or every other day. When asked, how could he be certain that the citizens were honest during their discussions, • as most would have been afraid? Hussein replied that this could have been the case, but he had a extremely long relationship with the Iraqi people and the population knew he sought the truth. Hussein gave an example involving his half-brother, Waban Ibrahim Hasan Al-Majid, the Minister of Interior at the time. A citizen reported to Hussein that while stopped at a traffic light, Waban fired his pistol at the traffic light. Hussein contacted Waban to determine if this was true. Waban acknowledged it was. Hussein then told him to pack his things, allowing him to learn of his removal. From Hussein instead of the state news radio. Hussein claimed that he held his family at a higher standard than others.

Hussein indicated he was interested in understanding the American culture, and did so by watching American movies. According to Hussein, he watched numerous American films, from these he developed his opinion of the American culture.

Saddam Hussein read a poem he recently wrote and I used this opportunity as a segue to discuss Hussein's Political speeches. I advised Hussein that after hearing several poems from him, I was now able to recognize Hussein's writing style, which was prevalent in a speech that I had recently read. It was clear to me that Hussein wrote his own speeches, which he confirmed further, stating all his writings came from the heart. Hussein claimed he did not enjoy reading his speeches, preferring instead to have his speeches read by others, such as news broadcasters. Hussein described the feeling of writing his speeches and giving them was the same as taking an exam.

I then asked Hussein if he wrote his own speeches and did they come from the heart, then what the meaning of his June 2000 speech was. Hussein replied this speech was meant to serve a regional and an operational purpose. Regionally, the speech was meant to respond to Iraq's regional threat. Hussein believed that Iraq could not appear weak to its enemies, especially Iran. Iraq was being threatened by others in the region and must appear able to defend itself. Operationally, Hussein was demonstrating Iraq's compliance with the United Nations {UN) in its destruction of its Weapons of Mass Destruction (WMD).

Hussein stated Iran was Iraq's major threat due to their common border and believed Iran intended to annex Southern Iraq into Iran. The possibility of Iran trying to annex a portion of Southern Iraq was viewed by Hussein and Iraq as the most significant threat facing Iraq. Hussein viewed the other countries in the Middle East as weak and could not defend themselves or Iraq from an attack from Iran. Hussein stated he believed Israel was a threat to the entire Arab world, not specifically Iraq.

Hussein continued the dialogue on the issues relating to the significant threat to Iraq from Iran. Even though Hussein claimed Iraq did not have WMD, the threat from Iran was the major factor as to why he did not allow the return of the UN inspectors. Hussein stated he was more concerned about Iran discovering Iraq's weaknesses. And vulnerabilities than the repercussions of the United States for his refusal to allow UN inspectors back into Iraq. In his opinion, the UN inspectors would have directly identified to the Iranians where to inflict maximum damage to Iraq. Hussein demonstrated this by pointing at his arm and stated striking someone on the forearm would not have the same effect as striking someone at the elbow or wrist, which would significantly disable the ability to use the arm. Hussein indicated he was angered when the United States struck Iraq in 1998. Hussein stated Iraq could have absorbed another United States strike for he viewed this as less of a threat than exposing themselves to Iran.

Hussein further stated that Iran's weapons capabilities have increased dramatically, while Iraq's have been eliminated by the UN sanctions. The effects of this will be seen and felt in the future, as Iran's weapons capabilities will be a greater threat to Iraq and the region in the future. Hussein stated Iraq's weapons capabilities were a factor in the outcome of the Iraq-Iran War. Initially during the war, Iraq had missiles with a limited range of approximately 270 Kilometers (km}, while Iran had no viable missile capability. The Iranians obtained long-range missiles from Libya which could strike deep into Iraq. The Iranians were the first to use the missiles, and struck Baghdad. Hussein claimed he warned the Iranians through a speech he gave, to cease these attacks. But the Iranians again attacked Baghdad. Iraq's scientists came to him and advised him that they could increase the range of Iraq's missiles to also reach deep into Iran. Hussein directed them to do so. Iraq responded to Iran's attacks by striking Iran's capital, Tehran, with its own missiles. Hussein stated the Iranians were up in arms to Iraq's strikes. Hussein stated that Tehran was more vulnerable to missile strikes due to its geographical design.

Baghdad, on the other hand, was geographically spread out and broken up into districts making Iran's missile strikes less effective. Hussein identified this as the "war of the cities" and Iraqi actions were in response to Iran's.   At that time, Hussein recognized that Iran was at a disadvantage, as Iraq had the technology to design and develop its missiles, while Iran was forced to obtain its missiles from Libya. Iraq was limited only by its own production while Iran was limited by the quantity it could obtain.

Hussein recognized that Iran continued to develop its weapons capabilities, to include its WMD, while Iraq had lost its weapons capabilities due to the UN inspections and sanctions. Hussein was asked how Iraq would have dealt with the threat from Iran once the UN sanctions were lifted. Hussein replied Iraq would have been extremely vulnerable to an attack from Iran, and would have sought a security agreement with the United States to protect it from threats in the region. Hussein felt such an agreement would not only have benefitted Iraq, but its neighbors, such as Saudi Arabia. I did agreed that such an agreement would have assisted Iraq immensely. I noted due to the history between the two countries, it would have taken some time before the United States would have entered into such an agreement with Iraq.

Further, I advised Hussein that paragraph 14 of UN Resolution 687 states that the disarming of Iraq was part of a total disarmament of the entire region, however, that portion of the resolution was not enforceable. The threat from Iran would have loomed over Iraq, especially as Iran had continued to advance its weapons capabilities. I commented that under those circumstances, it would appear that Iraq would have needed to reconstitute its own weapons program in response. Hussein replied that Iraq would have done what was necessary and agreed that Iraq's technical and scientific abilities exceeded others in the region.

Hussein commented he allowed the UN inspectors back into Iraq to counter allegations by the British Government.

Hussein stated this was a very difficult decision to make, but the British Government had prepared a report containing inaccurate intelligence. It was this inaccurate intelligence on which the United States was making their decisions. However, Hussein admitted that when it was clear that a war with the United States was imminent, he allowed the inspectors back into Iraq in hopes of averting war. Yet, it became clear to him four months before the war that the war was inevitable.

Hussein reiterated he had wanted to have a relationship with the United States but was not given the chance, as the United States was not listening to anything Iraq had to say. Further, he was concerned about the United States advanced technological capabilities and resources.

On another matter, Hussein stated he only recalls using the telephone on two occasions since March 1990.

Additionally, Hussein did not stay at the same location for more than a day, as he was very aware of the United States significant technological capabilities. Hussein communicated primarily through the use of couriers to communicate or would personally meet with government officials to discuss pertinent issues. Hussein stated that a technologically under-developed country, such as Iraq, was vulnerable to the United States.

The discussion then turned to the new interim President of Iraq, Sheikh Ghazi Al-Yawar. Hussein stated Al-Yawar came from a good family and would be favored by the other countries in the region, especially Saudi Arabia. Hussein stated it appeared the United States had put a lot of thought into Al-Yawar's appointment, as Al-Yawar was a good selection. I told Hussein the selection of Al-Yawar was not solely made by the United States, but was a joint effort by the United States and UN. The selection of the new Iraqi Government was based on the needs voiced by the Iraqi people. The new Iraqi Government has a strong foundation on which to build on as it progresses in its work to serve the Iraqi people. I then asked Hussein how he personally felt about their discussion of a new President and Government in Iraq. Hussein began to respond in reference to Al- Yawar, but I stopped him and asked how he personally felt. I reminded Hussein that he had previously made it clear to I that he still considered himself the President of Iraq. However, it is clear now to everyone hat he is no longer the President, as there is a new President who is representing the country and the people of Iraq. I told Hussein he is no, longer the President of Iraq; he was done. Hussein replied yes he knows, saying what he could do as it was God's choice. I asked him if he had any thoughts about his future and Hussein stated that it was in God's hands. I pointed out to Hussein that God was very busy and that God had more important issues than he and I. Hussein agreed, at which point, I told Hussein that his life is nearing its end, and asked him if he wanted the remainder of his life to have meaning, to which he responded yes.

I informed Hussein that he had surrounded himself with weak individuals, who are now refusing to take any responsibility for the actions of the former government. The other High Value Detainees were putting the blame for all of Iraq's mistakes on Hussein, to which Hussein replied by saying what could he do Hussein recognizes that he may bear the responsibility or blame while others will attempt to distance themselves.

Chapter 13

Casual Conversations Continued

Saddam Hussein stated on most days his work schedule consisted of meeting ordinary Iraqi citizens. Hussein preferred to meet them where they worked or lived instead of his office. Normally, Hussein tried to schedule time between 3:00 p.m. and 6:00 p.m. to interact with the Iraqi citizens. Hussein preferred to drive himself and would direct his protective detail to ride as passengers, which gave him the ability to stop whenever and wherever he wanted. Hussein took advantage of this time to address individual issues with citizens, which included discussions involving medical issues, personal grievances, etc.

Hussein enjoyed exchanging ideas with those around him for purposes of developing solutions. He encouraged those around him to discuss issues and exchange ideas amongst each other as well as with him. However, Hussein did not enjoy debating others, even though he considered himself an excellent debater, and superior to those around him. Whenever there were debates, Hussein stated he normally wouldn't take part, and would remain silent.

Hussein discussed individuals either related or close to him within the former Iraqi Government. Hussein stated Tariq Aziz (Black List #25) was very intelligent, and had the most knowledge regarding the West of all the Ba'ath Party officials. Aziz was an excellent speaker, as he was a former English teacher and former editor of .the Ba'ath Party newspaper.

Hussein stated Ali Hasan Al-Majid (Black List #5) thought like an Arab. I stated Al-Majid thought like a Bedouin, and Hussein stated that is what he meant to say. Al- Majid had limited experience outside of his tribe and his decisions were based on that limited experience. However, Al- Majid followed orders and carried out his duties as instructed.

Hussein described former Vice President, Taha Yasin Ramadan's (Black List #20) personality as open. Ramadan was the type of individual who continually talked about himself, which Hussein allowed him to do.

Hussein then discussed his two half-brothers, Barzan Ibrahim Hasan (Black List #38} and Waban Ibrahim Hasan (Black List #37} Hussein stated Barzan was very intelligent, but had a closed personality. I told Hussein that Barzan was not very friendly, and would not be the type of person with whom I could develop a friendship. Hussein laughed, and stated that I knew Barzan's personality. Hussein then stated Waban was the opposite of Barzan, friendly but simple.

According to Hussein, Waban could not carry out his Ministerial duties and was not capable of handling political positions or issues.

I inquired about Abid Hamid Mahmoud (Black List #4}, Hussein's Presidential Secretary.Hussein stated Abid was a good and loyal employee who carried out his duties and orders well. Hussein then asked me my opinion of Abid.

I described to Hussein the meaning of a "used car salesman. "Hussein again laughed and stated I was correct in his description of Abid.

I discussed with HUSSEIN Iraq's relationship with Al-Qaeda. HUSSEIN provided a brief historical account of conflicts between religion, specifically Islam, and historical rulers. HUSSEIN stated that he was a believer in God but was not a zealot. HUSSEIN believed that religion and government should not mix. Additionally, the Ba'ath Party ideology was not religiously based, as its founder was a Christian. However, HUSSEIN was clear that he opposed anyone who collaborated with the West against his country.

HUSSEIN stated USAMA BIN LADEN'S ideology was no different than the many zealots that came before him. The two did not have the same belief or vision. HUSSEIN claimed he had never personally seen or met Bin Laden. I advised HUSSEIN there is clear evidence the Iraqi Government had previously met with BIN LADEN. I specifically cited FAROUQ HIJAZI's (BL#104), former IIS M-4 Director, meeting with BIN LADEN in Sudan in 1994, ABU HAFS AL-MAURITANI's two visits to Baghdad, and his request for financial assistance of ten million dollars.HUSSEIN replied "yes". HUSSEIN stated the Iraqi government did not cooperate with BIN LADEN. I asked HUSSEIN "why not" since Iraq and BIN LADEN had the same enemies, United States and Saudi Arabia. I then cited him the quote "my enemy's enemy is my brother". HUSSEIN replied that the United States was not Iraq's enemy, but that HUSSEIN opposed its politics. If he wanted to cooperate with the enemies of the United States, HUSSEIN would have with North Korea, which he claimed to have a relationship with, or China. HUSSEIN stated that the United States used the 9/11 attack as a justification to attack Iraq. The United

States had lost sight of the cause of 9/11.I advised HUSSEIN that due to Iraq's contradiction between its statements and actions, many believe Iraq miscalculated the effects of the 9/11 attack on the American people and its leaders. Iraq denied having any connection with BIN LADEN or Al-Qaeda, but evidence showed continued contact between the two. HUSSEIN denied miscalculating the effects of the attack, but he did not have any options in front of him. The only choice he was given was to leave Iraq which he claimed was not an option.

I asked HUSSEIN why was Iraq the only country to applaud the 9/11 attack, which HUSSEIN immediately denied. I advised HUSSEIN that the Iraqi newspapers were reported to have applauded the attack. HUSSEIN stated that he wrote editorials against the attack, but also spoke of the cause which led men to commit these acts. The cause was never reviewed which could create such hatred to kill innocent people. After the attack, TARIQ AZIZ wrote personal letters denouncing the attack to two individuals, one possibly Ramsey Clarke, which AZIZ personally knew. These letters served as informal means of communications for Iraq to denounce the attack. HUSSEIN stated he could not make any formal announcement as Iraq considered itself at war with the United States. HUSSEIN was asked if that was why the request of the Iraqi Ambassador to the United Nations, MUHAMMAD AL-DURI, to attend the 9/11 memorial was denied by the Council of Four. It took the Minister of Foreign Affairs' personal request to HUSSEIN to obtain permission for the ambassador to attend the memorial. HUSSEIN stated he could not recall what transpired, but specifically remembered the ambassador attending the memorial. Again, HUSSEIN stated that the ambassador attended the memorial as a representative of the United Nations, and would not have attended as a formal representative of Iraq.

Chapter 14

This is a letter from Saddam Hussein to the Iraqi People and the Arab Nation written on his Birthday on April 28, 2003. The letter is in its entirety.

In the name of Allah,
The Compassionate, the Merciful:
'Indeed, [before the battle began] they swore
An oath to Allah that they would not turn back
In flight, and an oath to Allah must needs be
Answered for' [1]
Iraq, April 28, 2003

"From Saddam Hussein to the Great Iraqi People, and the Sons of the Arab and Islamic Nation, and men of honor everywhere: Peace be upon you, and Allah's mercy and blessings."

'This Is No Victory as Long as there is Resistance in Your Hearts'

"Just as Hulagu entered Baghdad, so did the criminal Bush enter Baghdad, with the help of [traitor from within] 'Alqami [2] indeed, even more than one 'Alqami."

"They did not vanquish you, you who refuse to accept occupation and humiliation, and you, who have Arabism and Islam in your hearts and minds, [they did not defeat you] except through treachery."

"By Allah, this is no victory, as long as there is resistance in your hearts."

"What we used to say has now become fact. We do not live in peace and security as long as the monstrous Zionist entity is on our

Arab land, and therefore there should be no split in the unity of Arab struggle."

"Oh sons of our great people, rise up against the occupier and do not put your trust in those who speak of Sunnis and Shiites, because the only problem that the homeland, your great Iraq, is experiencing now is occupation."

"There are no priorities [now] other than the expulsion of the cowardly, murderous infidel occupier. No honorable hand would be extended to shake his, except that of traitors and collaborators."

"I say to you that all the countries surrounding you are against your resistance – but Allah is with you, because you are fighting disbelief and defending your rights."

'The traitors have allowed themselves to proclaim their treachery, although this is a shameful thing. You should now proclaim your rejection of the occupier for the sake of the great Iraq and the nation, and for Islam and humanity."

"Iraq shall triumph, and with it the sons of the nation and men of honor. We shall restore the archeological artifacts they stole, and we shall rebuild Iraq that they want to divide into separate parts, may Allah bring shame upon them."

Palaces Not Registered In My Name – I Moved to a Small House Long Ago

"Saddam had no property registered in his own name and I challenge anyone to prove that the palaces were not registered in the name of the Iraqi state. I abandoned them long ago and went to live in a small house."

"Forget everything and resist occupation. The sinful error begins when there are priorities other than the occupier and his expulsion. Remember that they aspire to bring in the conflicting parties so that your Iraq will remain weak, so they can plunder it as they have been doing."

"Your Party, the Party of the Arab Socialist Ba'ath, is proud that it has not extended its hands to the Zionist enemy and did not make concessions to the cowardly American or British aggressor."

"Whoever stands against Iraq and plots against it shall not enjoy peace relying on American support."

"Blessings to every man of the resistance, every honorable Iraqi citizen, and to every woman, child, and elderly person in our great Iraq."

"Unite and the enemy will flee from you, and with him the traitors that entered with him."

"Know that he who came with the invading forces and he whose planes flew in order to kill you will not send you anything but poison."

"Allah willing, the day of liberation and victory will come, for us, for the nation, and for Islam above all else. This time, as always when right triumphs, the days to come will be better."

"Safeguard your property, your departments, and your schools, and boycott the occupier. Boycott him, as this is your duty towards Islam, the religion, and the homeland."

"Long Live Great Iraq and its people,"

"Long Live Palestine, free and Arab from the river to the sea,"

"Allah Akbar"

"Disgrace upon the despicable ones."

> "Saddam Hussein
> 26 Safar, 1424
> April 28, 2003"

Chapter 15

A quick overview of the History of Saddam Hussein.

Saddam Hussein, the son of a landless peasant, was born in Tikrit in 1937. His father died before his birth and the family lived in extreme poverty until his mother, Sabha, took a third husband, Hassan Ibrahim. His step-father was extremely stick and he was regularly beaten with an asphalt-covered stick. In turn, Saddam also became very cruel. At first to animals but in his teens he murdered a shepherd from a nearby tribe.

Tikrit was an area controlled by Sunni Muslims. Orthodox Sunni Arabs are only about 15% of Iraq's population and are completely outnumbered by the Shias in the south (approximately 60%) and the Kurds in the north. However, the Sunnis dominated Iraq's political life. The Sunnis also provided a disproportionate number of the country's military officers.

In 1955, Saddam went to live with his uncle in Baghdad and was educated at Karkh High School. in 1957 joined the Ba'ath Party, a radical, pan-Arab nationalist doctrine. During this period he became a street-gang leader that was opposed the British-created Hashemite monarchy.

In July 1958, King Faisal II and his entire household were assassinated during a military coup. Nuri es-Said attempted to escape from Baghdad disguised as a woman but he was captured and executed on 14th July, 1958.

As a result of the Iraqi Revolution, the Arab nationalist, Abdul Karim Kassem, became the country's new leader and in 1959 Iraq withdrew from the Baghdad Pact. Later that year Saddam Hussein was forced to flee to Egypt after being implicated in the attempted assassination of Kassem.

Kassem's moderate policies lost him the support of the Ba'ath Party and he was executed after a military coup in February 1963. Colonel Abd al-Salam Aref became the new president and Ahmad Hasan al-Bakr served as prime minister. As well as nationalizing the oil industry the new government developed close links with Gamal Abdel Nasser and his government in Egypt. Ahmad Hasan al Bakr left the government later that year when right-wing military leaders ousted the Ba'ath Party from power. Saddam Hussein, who was by this time the leader of Jihaz al-Hunein, was imprisoned and was not released until 1966.

When Abd al-Salam Aref was killed in an air crash on 13th April 1966 he was replaced by his brother General Abdul Rahman. Another military coup on 17th July 1968 brought to power Ahmad Hasan al-Bakr. He quickly nationalized the Iraq Petroleum Company and introduced wide-ranging social and economic reforms.

Over the next ten years Saddam Hussein held several important political posts in the government. This included Deputy Chairman of the Revolutionary Command Council (1968-1979). The Ba'ath Party government ruthlessly suppressed opposition but it did agree to enter negotiations with the Kurdish Democratic Party (KDP). In March 1970 the government promised to grant the Kurds a degree of autonomy.

On 6th October 1973, Egyptian and Syrian forces launched a surprise attack on Israel. Two days later the Egyptian Army crossed the Suez Canal while Syrian troops entered the Golan Heights. Iraq joined in the Arab-Israeli War but was defeated when Israeli troops counter-attacked on 8th October. Iraq was able to hurt the Western economy when it participated in the oil boycott against Israel's supporters.

It now became clear to the Kurdish Democratic Party that Ahmad Hasan al-Bakr was not going to keep his promises about Kurdish autonomy. In the spring 1974 fighting broke out between the Kurds and the government's armed forces. In March 1975 Iran closed its

121

border with Iraq which led to the collapse of the Kurdish military force. Kurdish villages were destroyed and their inhabitants resettled in specially constructed villages surrounded by barbed wire and fortified posts.

Ahmad Hasan al-Bakr also suppressed non-Kurds in Iraq. In July 1978 a decree was passed which made all non-Ba'thist political activity illegal and membership of any other political Party punishable by death for all those who were members or former members of the armed forces.

Saddam Hussein gradually increased his power in the Ba'ath Party and when Ahmad Hasan al-Bakr retired in July 1979, he became the new president. In the next few months Saddam Hussein swiftly executed his political rivals. Increasing oil revenues allowed him to increase spending on the building of schools, hospitals and clinics. He also established a literacy project that won him a Unesco award.

Another important reform was a massive program to bring electricity to Iraq. This was followed by a huge nationwide distribution of free fridges and television sets. He also improved the status of women and by the late 1970s they were a major part of the workforce.

A student of dictators such as Joseph Stalin and Adolf Hitler, Saddam Hussein arranged for portraits and statues to be placed all over the country. He also created the Republican Guard, an elite presidential security force.

In 1980 Saddam Hussein launched a war against Iran in an attempt to gain control of the Shatt al Arab Waterway that runs along the border of both countries. During the war Iraq received support from the United States, the Soviet Union, Britain and France.

In an effort to gain their independence from Iraq, the Kurds supported Iran during the war. Saddam Hussein retaliated and in the spring of 1988 the Iraq air force responded with poison gas, causing 5,000 deaths. As a result of these raids thousands fled to Turkey.

Iran gradually gained the upper-hand and recovered all its conquered territory and moved into Iraq and attempted to turn it into the world's second "Islamic Republic". Fearing that Iran would now dominate the region, the United States provided Saddam Hussein with conventional weapons, and the means to manufacture nuclear, chemical and biological weapons.

Iraq agreed to a cease-fire in July 1988. It is estimated that the Iraq-Iran War caused the deaths of 400,000 deaths and around 750,000 seriously injured. Of these casualties, three-quarters were Iranian.

Disillusioned by his rule, a group of soldiers in the Iraq Army attempted to overthrow Saddam Hussein in December 1989. The military coup failed and Saddam Hussein ordered the execution of 19 senior army officers.

It is estimated that Saddam Hussein spent around $5 billion a year on military rearmament. This created serious economic problems and began to consider the possibility of capturing the Rumelia oilfield in northern Kuwait. On 2nd August 1990 he ordered an invasion of Kuwait.

The United Nations immediately impose economic sanctions on Iraq and demanded an immediate withdrawal from Kuwait. In January 1991 a United States led coalition of 32 countries launch an attack on Iraq. Operation Desert Storm is a great success and after Iraq left Kuwait President George H. W. Bush was able to declare a cease-fire on 28th February.

In April 1991 Saddam Hussein agreed to accept the UN resolution calling on him to destroy weapons of mass destruction. He was also forced to allow UN inspectors into his country to monitor the disarmament. A no-fly zone was established in Northern Iraq to protect the Kurds from Saddam Hussein. The following year a no-fly zone was also created to protect the Shiite population living near Kuwait and Iran.

123

In April 1995, the UN Security Council passed an "oil-for-food" resolution. This allowed Iraq to export oil in exchange for humanitarian aid. However, this resolution was not accepted by Saddam Hussein until 1996.

The UN disarmament commission reported in October 1996 that Iraq continued to conceal information on biological and chemical weapons and missiles. Two months later Iraq suspended all cooperation with the UN inspectors.

In December 1998 the United States and Britain launched Operation Desert Fox, a four day intensive air strike that attempted to destroy Iraq command centres, missile factories and airfields. The following month U.S. and British bombers begin regular bombing attacks on Iraq. Over a 100 air strikes took place in 1999 and continued regularly over the next few years.

President George W. Bush described Iraq, Iran and North Korea as the "axis of evil" and made it clear that he intended to remove the governments of these three countries. In March 2003, Bush, with the support of Tony Blair, ordered the invasion of Iraq.

In December, 2003, following a tip-off from an intelligence source, US forces found Saddam Hussein hiding in an underground refuge on a farm near Tikrit. It was decided that Saddam should be charged with the massacre in the small town of Dujail in 1982. The trial began in October, 2005, but the proceedings were immediately adjourned.

A second trial on war crimes relating to the 1988 Anfal campaign opened in August, 2006. On 5th November, he was found guilty and the court sentenced him to death by hanging. The sentence was confirmed by Iraq's highest court and he was executed on 30th December, 2006.

References

All Noted References.

Interview Sessions 1 - 20 by SSA G.L. Piro | February 7th 2004 - May 1st, 2004

Letter to the People by Saddam Hussein | April 28th 2006 - Referenced topics below.

[1] Koran 33 (Chapter Al-Ahzab):15

[2] Mu'ayyad Al-Din Muhammad ibn Al-'Alqami was the vizier of the last Abassid caliph Al-Must'asim. Ibn Al-'Alqami reportedly assisted the Mongol army led by Hulago to take Baghdad in 1258.

Casual Conversations Interview by SSA G.L. Piro | May10[th] 2006 – June 28th, 2006

Printed in Great Britain
by Amazon